FLASHBACK

To: Colusa County Library
Best Wishes,
Ron Lewis

FLASHBACK

THE UNTOLD
STORY OF
LEE HARVEY
OSWALD

BY RON LEWIS
INTRODUCTION BY LESSIE R. YOUNG COLOMA

Flashback: The Untold Story of Lee Harvey Oswald
By Ron Lewis
Introduction by Lessie R. Young Coloma

Copyright © 1993 by Ronald LaVore Lewis
ISBN 1-883305-00-4

Published by
Lewcom Productions
P.O. Box 2429
Roseburg, OR 97470

DIRECT ALL INQUIRIES TO
Ron Lewis
PO Box 158
Winchester, OR 97495

94B4967

Book design and production by
Blue Heron Publishing, Hillsboro, Oregon.

Cover photograph courtesy of J.F.K. Assassination Information Center.

Printed and bound in the United States of America

10 9 8 7 6 5 4 3 2
First editon

INTRODUCTION

By Lessie R. Young Coloma

When Ron Lewis first approached me to act as editor and collaborator for his book, *Flashback, The Untold Story of Lee Harvey Oswald,* my first reaction was, "Oh, no; not another book on the assassination!" I was aware that a number of books had already been published on the subject, and I was afraid the public just might not be ready for another one yet. I figured anything connected with the assassination would be old news by now and that most persons would be weary of hearing about it. However, after sitting down and carefully discussing the matter with Mr. Lewis, I began to look at things in a different perspective. I realized he had information the world was entitled to. Here was a man who had been a close friend and companion of the one accused of killing the president of the United States, John Fitzgerald Kennedy, and he had something new to offer on the subject of Lee Harvey Oswald and the assassination… facts that had never before been revealed. There were various things he told me that added up, and I became convinced that this man was speaking the truth. "Why would a man want to implicate himself in something of such a serious nature if it were not true?" I thought. If the story were fraudalent it would hardly be worth taking the risk, as I saw it. It would not make sense for anyone to fabricate an account that would make him a subject of ridicule by the world, as well as a possible target for some deranged lunatic or patriotic fanatic.

After minimal consideration I agreed to take the job. I could see how desperately the author wanted to finish the book after years of laboring so diligently on it. Besides, from the short time we spent together while discussing the matter, I had already come to believe in his cause. Mr Lewis had experienced numerous problems and much frustration from the moment he decided to reveal things he had kept hidden for years. Like others who had knowledge of events connected to the assassination… he was met with a great deal of skepticism and ridicule. Yet he was determined to defend his account related in this book, and not deprive the public of vital information they had a right to have access to.

During our first appointment I saw that the manuscript had the potential for becoming an outstanding book, perhaps even a bestseller, with the wealth of information it contained. However, I had to agree with Ellen Ray of Sheridan Square Press, who informed Mr. Lewis that it needed a "vast amount of rewriting, reworking and editing." Oliver Stone had submitted the manuscript to the publishing company in behalf of its author, but at the time it was in its rough stages.

I was aware that the job represented a great deal of hard work, and that it would be several months at best before it would be ready to submit to the publishers. But I was excited about the challenge, and was looking forward to being involved in it! The more I got to know the author, the more I saw just how dedicated he was to getting the book finished. "The people have a right to this information," he told me. "It has been held back long enough." Oliver Stone also made the statement..."This book is evidence, and should be published."

As Mr. Lewis and I reviewed the manuscript, I learned that he had been incarcerated in April 1952 at the age of eighteen. After he was released in July 1954, he lived...according to his own words... "as a high-class bum." He never developed any roots and later became a fugitive, so he was "on the lam" when he met Lee Harvey Oswald in Dallas in October 1962. He met Lee again in New Orleans in August 1963, where they were associated until October 11 of that year. After the assassination Mr. Lewis went into hiding, eventually ending up in Del Rio, Texas, where he lived under an assumed name for about eight years before returning to Oregon in 1972. Most of his family had already given him up for dead, and it seemed like a miracle when he returned home.

I saw a printout of the author's FICA earnings from the Social Security records. It showed that his wages from the time of the assassination until 1982 were very sketchy. There was no income from 1963 till 1972 while he was in hiding, since he lived under an assumed name and existed by doing odd jobs. This was consistent with his story, and showed that the shock of the assassination had devastated his life to such an extent that he was never able to get back into the mainstream of employment.

When I interviewed his mother and sister in November 1992 Mrs. Lewis related, "Everyone told me throughout the years that my son was dead, because if he were alive he would have contacted us. I never believed it, though...I always knew in my heart he was alive. It was the most wonderful moment in my life when he came home!" His sister told me, "I was shocked and surprised to hear from him again after ten years." During all the years he was missing, they had "gone through every channel" in their efforts to locate him...even contacting the FBI.

During the course of editing the manuscript, the author would occasionally remember something from his past that had been pushed back deep into the recesses of his mind. I began to appreciate more and more his truthfulness and sincerity as all the information gradually came together, like pieces of a giant jigsaw puzzle. One thing that adds to the credibility of his account is that he revealed certain things he preferred to keep concealed, simply because he felt they had to be told. There are facts Mr. Lewis brings out about himself that do not put him at the best advantage, but he relates them truthfully and without pulling any punches.

A number of things will be brought out in this book that will prove the authenticity of his story. One such incident was alluded to by Oliver Stone during the program, "JFK Conspiracy-Final Analysis," broadcast from Washington, D.C. in March, 1992...a show that Mr. Lewis also appeared on. Stone stated that Marina Oswald Porter remembered an encounter with the author in front of the Crescent City Garage in New Orleans in 1963, which proves the truthfulness of his account. Nobody knew about the incident except the two of them.

When Mr. Lewis acted as technical advisor to Oliver Stone during the filming of the movie, "JFK," he associated with Stone in Dallas and New Orleans, researching and advising in connection with the movie. This served a twofold advantage, as it also provided us with additional research useful to the completing of this book.

This publication brings out who really killed President

Kennedy and what the motives were behind his death. It alludes to many of the clandestine activities connected with the assassination, and presents a different side of Lee Harvey Oswald. The truth is revealed about where Oswald really was on October 11, 1963 when he was supposed to have stayed in his room all day at Mrs. Bledsoe's rooming house in Dallas. The book also tells about Oswald's much-publicized change-of-address card, and shows who actually filled it out and deposited it in the post office in New Orleans. The truth is brought out about the two young boys in a late-model Ford that were at the scene of the Walker shooting. Also, there are some interesting facts revealed in connection with the photograph of Lee's father that disappeared right after Lee received it from his aunt...a photo that was never seen again.

During the course of preparing the "Flashback" manuscript for publication, we experienced several setbacks. We discovered that additional research was necessary, as well as encountering other things that had not been anticipated. In June 1992 I was in a serious automobile accident on Interstate 5, which delayed the work for over a month. The following August a runaway truck plowed into the author's mobile home, devastating a huge section, and eventually hospitalizing him with a heart attack. There were also other setbacks that caused additional delays, but we knew we had to meet a deadline. So we continued to burn the midnight oil and were eventually able to finish the worthwhile project, which I feel privileged to have had a part in.

In my opinion this is the most in-depth book ever written about Lee Harvey Oswald, and will be a valuable contribution to the historical record. It covers various aspects of Oswald's life, and reveals a private side of his complex personality that only someone who was very close to him could present to the populace. It provides a true picture of Oswald as he really was, and was written by a man who knew him personally.

ACKNOWLEDGEMENTS

I am indebted to the following individuals, listed in alphabetical order, for their contributions to this book:

Lessie R. Young Coloma, Mary Ferrell, Larry Harris, Gerry Hemming, Larry Howard, Marie H. Kemp, Priscilla McMillan, Marina Oswald Porter, Gary Shaw, and Oliver Stone. Lastly, I am indebted to my mother, Gwynethe Lewis, who put up with me all my life and helped labor over this book for four years.

Besides knowing Lee Harvey Oswald, one of the highlights of my life was serving as technical advisor for Oliver Stone in the movie, "JFK". I am also grateful for the privilege of working with Gary Oldman, Beata Pozniak, Joe Pesci, Ed Asner, Tommy Lee Jones, Kevin Costner, Kevin Bacon and those in the cast: Tina, Jane and the Camelot film crew. I appreciate the many new friends I made on the set.

I would like to extend a special thanks to those who encouraged me to write this book, as well as to Irvin Magri Investigative Services and staff for their consideration and hospitality. I shall never forget the kindness of those I met in Fort Worth, Dallas and New Orleans, while working on the set of "JFK", and I am most grateful that I had the opportunity to appear in televised interviews, such as "The JFK Conspiracy - Final Analysis," originating in Washington, D.C. in March 1992.

DEDICATED

to

JUNE AND RACHEL

Lovely daughters of my friend, Lee Harvey Oswald

FOREWORD

It is unlikely that a government which refuses to admit the existence of a conspiracy would try one for complicity in that conspiracy, as pointed out to me by researchers while I was being scrutinized by two FBI agents at a dinner party at the St. Regents Hotel in May 1991 in Dallas.

The uncertainties about the details surrounding the presidential assassination and Lee Harvey Oswald are fully justified, as I will show in this book.

At the Rosehill cemetery in Fort Worth, Texas, there is a gravestone that merely says OSWALD, delineating the grave of Lee Harvey Oswald, accused assassin of the President of the United States, John Fitzgerald Kennedy. The men that hurriedly dug that grave were told by Secret Service agents that a William Bobo was to be buried there, perhaps for fear that they would refuse to dig a grave for the accused assassin of President Kennedy.

In corresponding with Priscilla Johnson McMillan, she advised that writing this book would probably not bring me any happiness, but she said, "...if you can contribute to the understandive of Oswald, then I hope you will do it." McMillan was a former Kennedy employee who had interviewed Lee Oswald when he was a defector in the Soviet Union, and later wrote the Marina Oswald biography, entitled *Marina and Lee*.

The inconsistencies in the assassination story and the skepticism I have experienced about my testimony, give some insight into the plight that conspiracy survivors face. Out of this segment of people, occasionally one such as myself or Roscoe White will surface, but the contribution they are able to make to the record is shrouded with uncertainty. As we endure such skepticism, we are hypothesized as mentally disturbed or as liars. I feel I must address this situation because there are some seeking recognition, who resort to hoaxes. Those researchers piecing the dilemma together are faced with the complexity of deciding what is fiction and what is fact. On the other hand, those who are coming out in public about the assassination after such a long period of silence, face the arduous task of verifying the information.

Some individuals have escaped detection by covering the tracks that led to the assassination so convincingly that it is sometimes difficult to reconstruct connections with concrete proof. We become accustomed to skepticism and learn to deal with it. If abundant proof linked us with the incident, we would have been discovered long ago. Some of us who were more directly involved have held out for a reason, moreso than those superficially involved; we have had more to conceal, so now we have more to say.

In my haste to cover my tracks, I destroyed a photograph of Lee and myself taken at the New Orleans Greyhound bus terminal. During the latter part of August I cut the photo in half, sending the part that contained my picture to a girl in Harlengen,

Texas. The other half I threw in the trash can after the assassination. I also destroyed my diary, a picture of General Walker's house and documented addresses of Lee's acquaintances, Ruth Payne and David Ferrie. If I had saved those items, I would have less of a problem verifying my case today, but I was desperate to destroy anything that showed any connection to Lee and the other conspirators!

For those of you who feel you would have handled things differently, there's an old saying that goes, "Everyone knows what to do with the bull except the one who has him by the tail." Had I come forward, my story would be old news by now, because I would have already been interrogated in the initial reports. Without my testimony the missing pieces of the puzzle may never be found. If everyone having bits and pieces of information would come forward, the puzzle could be completed. An article demonstrating this reasoning appeared in the December 22, 1989 issue of *Awake Magazine*, as follows:

FILLING THE GAPS

It can be said that death is one of the greatest enemies of truth, since people take to their graves information that no other humans know. The exact details of even comparatively recent events for example, the 1963 assassination of the president of the United States, John Fitzgerald Kennedy...are still a matter of controversy. What are the facts? Who really knows? Many who might know are no longer alive. And if this is true of an event only 26 years in the past, what about events that took place hundreds or even thousands of years ago?

*22 Dec. 1989 *Awake Magazine*.
25 Columbia Heights, Brooklyn, NY 11201

DEADLINE

CHAPTER I

In August 1963, I was informed that President Kennedy was going to be assassinated. Yes, I had prior knowledge of the tragedy, but failed to give it the attention required in time to save his life. This is something I have lived with for three decades. It has stayed with me continually, tormenting me day in and day out, a constant reminder of the part I played in the assassination of John F. Kennedy, by remaining silent when I should have spoken up.

The tragic consequence of my negligence hit me like a ton of bricks on November 22, 1963, as I listened to radio reports of the assassination. I was horrified! I had procrastinated, and now it was too late. Kennedy was dead! Oh, why hadn't I spoken up when it might have done some good? Why didn't I tell someone about the plot to assassinate him before it happened? I knew the men who had conspired to kill the president, and perhaps I could have informed the proper authorities of the conspiracy in time to save his life. But I guess I just never thought it would really happen. The justification that made it possible to live with this secret for so many years without revealing it, was that I had convinced myself there was nothing I could do about it now. The president was dead and if I revealed what I knew, I would no doubt be killed, too, along with dozens of others who were in some way connected to the assassination.

So, I had known Lee Harvey Oswald! Why should I tell the whole world about it? My life was semi-private and I liked it that way. I enjoyed indulging in many of the small pleasures that most people take for granted, such as going to the local cafe every morning for coffee. I had few friends, but I appreciated the ones I had and enjoyed their company. Simple things I found pleasurable, such as taking a walk in the rain, or feeling the warmth from the sun. I was afraid I would be deprived of pleasures such as these if I told my story. I treasured my freedom, and had made a clean break from everything connected to the assassination, which was truly a remarkable accomplishment, considering how deeply I was involved. Little did I know of the skepticism I would meet when I finally decided to reveal what I knew!

Why change all of that now? I had distanced myself from the incident, a mental process that worked. I realize now that I was afraid to remember, thus, certain deep, dark secrets al-

A 1991 NEWSPAPER ARTICLE
THE ABOVE IS A 1991 ARTICLE ON MY INVOLVEMENT WITH LEE
HARVEY OSWALD. GETTING SUCH AN ARTICLE PUBLISHED IN
THE NINETIES IS NOT AN EASY TASK. HOWEVER, IT BECAME
EASIER AFTER MY INVOLVEMENT IN THE MOVIE, "JFK."

most remained locked away forever in the recesses of my mind. What circumstances could cause a man to come close to taking such monumental secrets with him to the grave?

Cautiously, I shared the information with friends and relatives, who advised me to keep my mouth shut and not get involved. They were afraid that my connection to the alleged assassin or conspirators would discredit our family in a way that could never be reversed, if it became common knowledge.

When I finally came out of hiding and returned to Oregon in 1972, my family was shocked and overjoyed! They hadn't heard from me for ten years and most of them had long ago given me up for dead; and now, like a miracle, I had returned! I was accompanied by my two young sons, Kenneth and Delbert Lee, who were born while I lived in Del Rio, Texas.

It seemed like a dream that after so many years I was home at last! The first day after arriving, my family and I had a lot of catching up to do. One matter of concern was that we all wanted to know for sure what risks were involved in my return. After all, I had known Lee Harvey Oswald, the accused assassin of the president, and my name was linked to his in the Banister files! My fears of being discovered dominated all my thoughts, and my family was afraid I would be arrested. Frankly, I didn't know what to expect, but now that I was home, it was important to know if I were a suspect in the assassination.

After reflecting on the matter, my two brothers, Delbert and Ewart, came up with a plan. The three of us drove to downtown Roseburg, and they went into the Douglas County Sheriff's Department to see what they could find out. Delbert, who bore a strong resemblance to me, pretended to be me and told them he was wanted by the FBI, which was his way of probing to see if I was on the wanted list. He did this on his own initiative, figuring that if he was arrested, he could eventually prove who he was, and be released. In that case, I would have gone back into hiding, leaving my children with my family.

While I waited in the car, all sorts of things flashed through my mind. "What if I'm on the list and have to continue living as a fugitive?" I worried. "Could I ever return to such an existence?" When my two brothers returned, I was relieved to find out I was not on the wanted list. In time I resumed a normal life, to the extent possible, and made every effort to put the past behind me.

When I first began toying with the idea of writing a book, I found that public interest in the assassination had diminished considerably since 1963. Some of the obstacles I was confronted with were the news media and publishers who were weary of stories dealing with the assassination. It was too late! I had missed the deadline!

In 1963, when any information concerning assassination witnesses was brought before the public, there wasn't the media resistance experienced today. I didn't anticipate skepticism. If I had, I am sure I would have told my story before the present era when a person's word, as a rule, could be relied upon. Since a lie seems to be, for the most part, more widely accepted today than the truth, the people have become skeptical. They have no way of knowing for sure if a story is factual or if it's just another false account, written by an author hoping to gain recognition or benefit financially, or whatever the motive might be. No matter how the populace responds to my story, it must be recorded as a valuable addition to the existing record.

I began keeping a diary in April 1962, but when I left New Orleans on November 27, 1963, I took it to Harlengen, Texas, where I burned the parts that connected me to Lee. Years later, I rewrote the diary with minimal coverage of my summer in New Orleans, and gave a copy to my brother in 1972. It has been stored in his safe since then, and contains only what I felt comfortable with keeping around.

BURIED ALIVE

CHAPTER II

In August 1963, Lee Oswald and I became friends. I was possibly the only real friend Lee ever had, and it is important to know who I was and why I was attracted to Lee.

Although my true name was Ron Lewis, I was using the alias, Ron Larson, at the time. I was a fugitive from justice, with a strong desire to remain free. To acquaint the reader with the man who befriended Lee that summer, I will give a brief rundown of my life from 1949 to 1962.

In June 1949, when Company M of the 144th Infantry of the 41st Division of the Oregon National Guard was having an enlistment drive, I had friends in the Guard and was impressed by the uniforms, the militarism and the association. I wanted to join and give my buddy, Joe Mays, the credit for my enlistment. However, I was only sixteen and it would be another month before I would be old enough. The days passed slowly, but finally on July 17, which seemed to take forever, I joined the Guard, feeling real important.

A year later the unit would move to summer camp at Fort Lewis, Washington, the source of many incidents my buddies told me about. Anxious for a taste of active duty, I transferred to the Air Force on December 28, 1949. I started out patriotic; all red, white and blue, but during a visit back home, an incident took place that would change the course of my life forever. My National Guard buddies fixed me up with a girl, who generously provided Company M with her favors. They promised she would be a cinch, which she was. Since I was pressed for time, I was happy they had provided me with an easy make for a one-night stand!

We went to a drive-in theater with another couple and my date's parents, all in the same car. Afterwards, we took her parents home, then the other couple, my date and I drove out into the country, and parked. She was so easy, that to a person of her caliber, a date wasn't a date unless it included sex, perhaps the assurance she needed to feel like a desirable female. Whatever the case, it would've been difficult not to have sex with this girl, since it was obviously her intent that it was included in the date. As strongly as she came on, there was no doubt in my mind that if one of us was overpowered, it was me!

The next morning when I was having breakfast in a downtown cafe called the Silver Grill, Milo, the deputy sheriff, ambled in, so I waved him over to my table. As I began telling him I was leaving later that day to return to the service, he interrupted. "Did you go out with a girl last night and have sex with her?" he asked.

"Sure did!" I told him. "You got a problem with that?"

"I'm sorry, Ron, but as soon as you finish your breakfast, I'm gonna have to take you down to the courthouse," Milo told me. "The girl's parents have pressed charges."

"But that little gal has had sex with lots of guys from Company M!" I protested.

"I know that, Ron," he said, sympathetically, "but I have no choice. I know the reputation that girl has, though, so you'll probably be out in no time."

I couldn't believe it! Her parents, suddenly intent on reforming their daughter, had turned me in, even though they had provided two cases of beer for our small party of four minors. "What a couple of hypocrites!" I thought, angrily. Being in the wrong place at the wrong time, I happened to be the guy who got the axe. I was mad as hell!

She was fourteen, and mature beyond her years. I was seventeen and in the military, therefore emancipated, so that constituted statutory rape in the State of Oregon. Yet, we were both minors, and although she was definitely a consenting minor, she wasn't yet sixteen, the age of consent in Oregon.

For this infraction of the law, I received a five-year suspended sentence, which caught up with me a few months later in the service. After a year and twenty-six days of active duty, I was given an undesirable discharge at the age of eighteen. Incidentally, this was upgraded to honorable in 1979, as ordered by the secretary of the Air Force.

After my discharge, I reported to the court for further action, as required. I received a reduced sentence and was placed on three years' active probation, which I failed to comply with. I found it difficult to adhere to rules and regulations of reporting while I was on probation, and was later sent to the Oregon State Prison in Salem for rule violation. There was no crime committed, just failure to report on time, or not reporting at all.

The prison was very old, in fact, ancient, and in the last several years it had been in the process of reconstruction. New cell blocks were being built, but there was one old block still remaining, the last one to be torn down. It was known as B Block, where I spent the first several months of my incarceration. The cell block consisted of badly decomposed bricks, which provided a glimpse of the length of time the prison had existed, and of the misery exacted upon its occupants for more than a century. Nowadays when you are imprisoned, you are incarcerated, but when you went to prison in the fifties, you were buried alive!

The cells were made of iron, welded and bolted together, five tiers in all. The bars on the doors were the old flat type, instead of the conventional round bars that eventually replaced them, as prison transition evolved. The doors were locked with an old-style padlock, and it was not uncommon for a prisoner to have a key to his cell. The doors didn't have automatic mechanisms such as the modern versions have. In order to open one door, a bar at the head of the stairs would be pulled and all the doors would tentatively open, awaiting the unlocking of the padlock on each individual cell. This process involved a great deal of clanking and echoing within the old structure.

There was a sink in the corner of each cell. It had a faucet that provided cold running water, used for washing one's hands and face, as well as providing drinking water. The sink was also used for urination, a situation I found unacceptable, although I was forced to live with it.

Each of the inmates was provided with a bucket that had a lid on it. It was commonly referred to as the "shit bucket," and there was a set time for carrying it out to a place where it was emptied and cleansed. At six-thirty every morning, as the noisy iron bar slid over the door and the padlocks on two-hundred doors were hurriedly unlocked by the convict detail, the shout rang out loudly, "Shit line! Shit line!" Many inmates would grab their buckets, step out the door and get in line, a daily ritual. The destination was an area where a little creek ran through the yard and the buckets' contents were dumped. This is how the creek acquired the name "Shit Creek," and is so called to this day.

To the convicts who had already integrated into the more modern structures, this procession was a primitive arrangement. It was dehumanizing for those still incarcerated there, causing shame and humiliation because the final phase of their digestive process had to be dealt with in such a barbaric, degrading manner.

The beds of B Block were made up of two half-inch water pipes stretched from one end of the cell block to the other, which ran the length of twenty cells. Bailing wire was criss-crossed from one pipe to the other, creating a type of make-shift bedspring. On top were straw mattresses that had been there for God only knows how long. Additional pipes were placed above the bed, creating a double bunk in each cell.

At the beginning of his term, each inmate was issued a foul-smelling army blanket, which was never washed during his period of confinement. The lifers were an exception. They would occasionally receive a clean blanket, perhaps once every couple of years. Fresh sheets were usually provided weekly, but we were never given a pillow.

The manner in which the bunks were constructed, afforded no real privacy for any of the inmates. For example, if someone made certain movements three or four cells down the line, the thin pipes would tell on him, and it could be determined just who it was by the velocity of the vibration. Needless to say, it created a problem in that environment of womenless men.

At eighteen I was what they called a "pink kid." The long-termers tried to make girls out of kids like these. I found this out the first night of my incarceration, when I realized I had a natural self-defensive streak in me that I was unaware of until then. They had put me in a cell with a thirty-seven-year-old named Willie, who was doing fourteen years for armed robbery. Suddenly, without warning, he came up behind me and began rubbing against my backside. I could tell he was sexually excited. As he made advances, I resisted and slammed his head against the bars, which resulted in a scar that was still on his face throughout the remainder of my term.

"What did you do that for?" he exclaimed. "All you had to do was say something!"

"When somebody does something like that, Willie, you slam 'em," I told him. Instead of continuing to harass me, he showed me some respect after that, and from then on, he considered me his friend. The next day he took me to the recreation department, and I was given a job where convicts were in control, with no guards to oversee them; certainly the envy of other inmates.

Evidently, Willie saw something in me that would be useful to the cause of the more hardened element. I was the only person in the recreational department that had less than fourteen years to do. Like I said, I was young and pink, but also tough, and for this reason, I would get along with the convicts and also maintain the respect of the guards.

Because of my comely and innocent looks, the guards weren't as apt to shake me down as they were the more hardened-looking element; and being a short-termer, I would receive a less suspicious eye from the guards.

My assignment would entail transporting contraband throughout the prison. My first job was to take a wheelbarrow filled with baseball mitts, from the office to a storage area in the prison cannery building. At the checkpoint the guard searched through the mitts for contraband. Then after the wheelbarrow was taken to the storage area and unloaded, it was filled with softball bases and returned to the office, where it was checked again for smuggled items. While at the office, it was loaded with softballs and returned to the inspection point, where nothing unusual was found. On the next load, the guard, weary of the incessant checking, waved me on through.

It was now time to bring in the contraband. As I came back through the checkpoint the wheelbarrow was empty, so when I passed a freight car close to the door, two one-hundred pound sacks of sugar slammed into it faster than the eye could catch it! I took the uncovered sugar to the office, where a number of heavy baseball bats were placed on top, then I went back through the point of inspection where the guard waved me through again.

The sugar was used in a prison alcoholic drink called pruno. This was the type of job I had for my first five months behind prison walls. I learned to make pruno well, and I invented a potent recipe, using pineapple juice and water. It was a well-protected secret, since I sold it for two cartons of cigarettes per gallon. The concoction would get a person drunk, and about a quart was all I ever drank at one time.

Billy Fritz, one of the inmates who was in a cell next to mine, made a wooden box which he tarred to keep from leaking, then put up a thirty-gallon batch of potato jack in it. The brew gave off an awful odor, and there was also a smell of pruno in the air continually. There were secret hiding places the guards never did discover, so they became accustomed to the smell, and simply resolved to live with the problem. With the scent of pruno in the air, we would sit innocently on the box that contained the brew, passing the time playing cards while the guard stood in a relaxed position at the door, watching our plays, waiting for his shift to end. My friend, Merle, would tell the guard, "I hope they find that garbage; it makes me sick!" This would throw suspicion off of us, although we were literally sitting on the stuff!

I noticed that even among the prison population, there was a sense of patriotism, but my circle of friends had other interests, and spent a lot of time daydreaming. It was a means of escape, without going through the physical motions. In those days there were no home leaves, as some prison programs now offer. There weren't any televisions or modern conveniences; just hard time to do!

Soon we had a communist cell going, and began to hold meetings. This was during the era when such radio programs as "I was a Communist for the FBI" were popular, and when the McCarthy hearings were in full-swing against the American Communist Party. We had earphones, and could make out two radio stations. This was our escape from reality and a way of opposing the establishment that had incarcerated us.

Some inmates opposed the idea of communism, and displayed a degree of patriotism. After considerable thought, I questioned how a person could accept being imprisoned in a place like that without resistance. I resented my incarceration very much, especially on such flimsy charges. My transfer from the status I enjoyed under the suspended sentence to the active probation program, had a ring of political football, and I was the football. Such was my circumstance, and I was unable to accept it. Although I couldn't foresee it at the time, I would receive a pardon from Governor Atiyeh of the State of Oregon in the year 1979.

I didn't understand all of this in my youth, but I realized something was amiss, and fought back any way I could. Joining the communist cell, I generally toyed with communism. At the prison library I obtained books on Russia and China, because they were communist countries. I read about the history of the Chinese revolution in a book called *Red Star Over China*, by Edgar Snow. I found It particularly interesting because it brought out the fact that China was engaged in a civil war, which was suspended to form a United Front against the invading Japanese forces, to be continued after Japan's defeat.

Because of my obvious disenchantment with the country that had incarcerated me, I developed subversive leanings, which would remain with me for many years. That encouraged me to get a better education, since I had never finished school. Eventually, I was able to attend school while in prison, after trying my hand at prison construction, a job that paid twenty-five cents a day in wages!

There was construction under way that would lead to

much-needed transitional programs to serve a more modern society. There were two new cell blocks being completed, and a steam tunnel was being dug from C Block to the new segregation building. It would not be long until ancient B Block would be torn down, and replaced with a modern structure. I stayed there until the jackhammers began their assault. If it were true, as I suspected, that demons lurk in such places, it was their last stand, and B Block was the last to fall, making way for a more modern prison.

One day they moved Willie to one of the new cell blocks and I was left all alone. Such an empty feeling for a boy of eighteen! It was the first time it actually dawned on me that everything around me wasn't just a dream. During my first few days in prison, I would wake up in the mornings, unaware of just where I was. But as my eyes began to adjust, I remembered, reluctantly, that I was in prison and would be there for a long time to come! The next three years seemed like an eternity!

Reuben, a young boy of fourteen, was sent to prison while I was doing time. There was no intermediate facility in Oregon in those days, and his age concerned the prison staff. They refused to place him in a cell with a hardened lifer where he wouldn't stand a chance in adjusting to the adult atmosphere. I could visualize the staff sitting around the table, trying to decide what they were going to do with the boy. Their decision was to place him in my cell. Although it was a gamble, they would sleep better at night, knowing they had tried to place him with the safest cell-mate. Now he might have a chance.

I was tough enough to hold my own against the hardened element, and hoped Reuben would be able to do the same. But it was easy to see there was going to be a problem with that kid holding his own against those weathered criminal types. For one thing, he had the features of a girl, which the lifers considered a bonus. I began to clue him in, while having high hopes that my efforts would be effective, happy that Reuben was so receptive. I visualized him foiling any attempts at conversion made by those lewd old guys who would be calling at our cell within an hour or two.

"Reuben, don't make the mistake of taking any candy or chewing gum when it's offered to you," I warned him, "and no matter how bad you want to smoke, don't take any tailor-mades from these cons. I have a sack of Bull Durham, and I'll give it to you. It's prison-issued and doesn't cost anything. And no matter what, don't take a pillow or pajamas either!" Hoping to instill in him a hint of what could be the outcome if he made such an unwise move, I added, "If you do, you'll end up over in C Block with a dress on and a ribbon around your head!"

Soon a couple of lifers showed up at the cell door, wearing neatly pressed pants and shirts, unlike the sloppy clothes most cons wore.

"Hey, Kid, want a cigarette?" one of the convicts asked.

"Sure," said Reuben.

"No, thanks!" I said, "He don't smoke!"

"Keep out of it, Louie; this is between Reuben and me. Want a light?" asked the lifer, striking a match and lighting the kid's cigarette.

Reuben fell for it, hook, line and sinker! I wanted to throttle him for being so dumb. He lost in the first round, convinced that prison was not such a bad place after all. Here it was his very first night, and he had already been given free candy and cigarettes, and even a pillow with little frills on it!

Disgusted, I sat down on my bunk and rolled a Bull Durham, proud of myself because it wasn't a tailor-made. A week later, I saw Reuben in the other Block in a cell that had curtains. He was wearing a dress. As the saying goes, "If you dance, you gotta pay the fiddler." The lifers had won!

I was excited about my new construction job! It was better than sitting around playing cards and keeping the pruno warm. I had been working in a trench that was going to be the steam tunnel. Digging in the rain-soaked dirt, I was relieved when a new detail became available at the segregation building. I volunteered for the job because I was sick and tired of wading knee-deep in the good old Oregon mud. Summer was gone and now the rain was here, just the time of year prison officials would decide to do this job! After all, we were here for punishment, and for them to arrange for us to do it at this particular time somehow seemed to be justified in the minds of those who planned the projects.

I had great plans for my new job. Not having to be in the ten-foot-deep muddy trench anymore, seemed like a much better deal. I didn't dream I would end up wishing I was back in the mud after rumors began circulating that we were going to build a gas chamber. That bothered me a great deal. I had already seen one man go to his death in the wooden gas chamber located over by the wall where the glass capsule was contained. The death of a man is not easy to watch, but perhaps if he were sick or in pain it would be more acceptable. It was difficult for me to agree that the death penalty was a feasible final solution. I realized it was an accepted form of punishment where men sit in judgement, but even at the early age of eighteen, I knew I could not be a part of it.

Long, one of the guys on death row, had killed a guard. He

was young and healthy, only in his twenties. On the morning he was to be executed he passed up his last meal and just sat on his bunk staring into space, occasionally puffing on a cigarette. "My god!" I thought, "Who in hell would feel like eating at a time like that anyway!" When the guards came for him, Long took a few more puffs on his cigarette before they took him away. As soon as he got outside he flipped the cigarette onto the ground, then walked into the little green building. As I watched from the fifth tier of B Block, I felt that it was probably a relief for a man who had been incarcerated since his seventeenth birthday to finally be leaving that hell-hole. But we have no way of knowing for sure exactly how one feels in a situation like that until we actually sit in the chair ourselves, and this I would eventually do while still in prison. Before my time was up, I saw two more men meet the same fate as Long.

At the job site, we picked up our shovels, ready to dig into our work. However, there was something that bothered me intensely, so I asked the boss, "Scotty, what are we making here?"

"A gas chamber," he replied.

Everyone else started digging in their assigned places, but I fiddled around with the shovel handle for a few seconds and was beginning to look conspicuous, like I might have been gold-bricking. The others kept telling me, "Get going, Luke, Scotty has his eye on you!"

"I don't know about you guys, but I just can't work on the gas chamber," I said. For a moment the demons cringed, as our work detail came to a halt, two of the guys laying down their shovels with me. After this, my friend Merle and I were known as the "Gold Dust Twins" because we always looked for reasons to get out of working.

Scotty said, "If you guys don't get to work, I'm gonna write you up." Refusing to comply, I walked over to a concrete slab and sat down, waiting for whatever was to come. The guys pleaded for me to get to work! I was a popular convict because I was always in the middle of something and everyone wanted to be like me. I knew the guys were concerned about me, but I just couldn't bring myself to work on the gas chamber. Even though I knew it was in my best interest to cooperate, my body just would not respond!

I was the only one in the work crew to be taken to the hole. I had never been there before, but had heard all kinds of horror stories about what went on. One thing I knew was that they held a kangaroo court in the basement of C Block, where they sentenced you, and then a guard held each arm while Captain Herder would punch out your stomach. He had cold, steel-gray eyes that could burn a hole right through you with his penetrating stare. I wondered, was this method supposed to be some kind of educated theory, far above my level of understanding, that was used to rehabilitate men?

Captain Herder, glancing at the write-up in front of him, queried, "Refusing to work, eh?"

"I refuse to work on the gas chamber," I answered.

"Does that bother you?" he asked.

"Yes, it bothers me, because I don't have any blood on my hands and I don't want to start now," I told him.

"You're very young to make a decision like that," he said. "Are you prepared to suffer for it?" I told him I was. "Six days in the hole!" he ordered. Two guards grabbed me by the arms as I closed my eyes. Knowing I couldn't get out of this one, at least I didn't have to watch. As I tried to distance myself from reality, I could hear Herder putting on his famous kid-leather gloves.

"Open your eyes!" he demanded. Boring a hole through me with his icy stare, he ordered, "Put him in a cell." Was there some decency left in Captain Herder, after all? I had never heard of a man going to the hole without receiving a beating first. I just couldn't believe my good luck!

The cell was dark, but had some light coming from a small window in the corridor. There was probably a total of ten cells in all, with about half of them occupied by naked prisoners. Was I about to learn firsthand how men are rehabilitated and reshaped into decent, obedient citizens?

The boy in the cell with me was a fifteen-year-old named Roger, who was sent to the hole for some infraction that escapes me now. As I took off my clothes to hand to the guard, Roger whispered, "Keep a button!" Trusting that there was a reason, I tore one from my shirt and heard it fall to the floor, bouncing around lightly before it came to a halt. It was the first time in my life I remembered experiencing dead silence. You could have heard a pin drop.

The iron door in the corridor went "clank!" as the guard left, closing it behind him. There was a toilet in the cell, but no paper. We didn't have any water, blankets, or mattresses. There was only the button and a concrete floor. We were in "no man's land!"

Roger and I used the button for a game. We would spin around, throw the button, and see who could find it first. As we grew tired of the game and the dim light from the little window in the corridor began fading into total darkness, we heard the clanking of the steel door. It was a sound that I would never get used to. It signaled suppertime, which was cold oatmeal and water, nothing else. The same rations twice a day!

We slept cold and naked on the concrete floor, and I was beginning to understand what it was like to be an animal. We were no longer men. Stripped of our dignity, we were treated like the lowest form of creation. The long days passed slowly. It felt like we were buried about as deep as a human could be and yet still be among the living. I soon noticed a door that food was taken through, bypassing us. So this was isolation! I had heard of it, a place where people who could not adjust to the general population, were kept in protective custody. They were able to have tobacco, matches, cigarette papers and decent food. After a couple of days of cold oatmeal it just killed me to smell that good food going by my cell. I began to realize how a hungry dog must feel, waiting for a scrap to fall to the floor.

Soon we saw a button with a string tied to it make an appearance under the steel door. One of the guys managed to grab hold of it, then he started pulling it, see-sawing it up about three inches, continuing to pull until a piece of sheet appeared. Because the door had been sprung enough to accommodate it, a tightly-rolled sheet came through, containing tobacco, matches, an object to strike them on and some papers so we could roll our own. When the guards came in with the cold oatmeal, they would smell smoke and search the cells, usually finding some of the stuff. One guard exclaimed, "How the hell do they manage to get that junk in here? It's absolutely impossible!" But he had forgotten that we were still human, with the ability to reason and devise ingenious ways of improvising. He figured that when people are locked down, that's the end of it.

It occurred to me that the guards suspected each other of slipping the smokes in. However, it would have been a black mark on their record for not being on top of it, so it wasn't reported to their supervisor, and had probably gone on this way for a century! The situation reminded me of brewing pruno in B Block. Finally, on the sixth day, after what seemed like an eternity, a guard came in and handed me a razor with a Star razor blade in it. He told me to shave because I was going to court. I never could shave with one of those prison-issued single-edged blades. To make matters worse, I hadn't shaved for six days, and had nothing but cold water and no soap, so I decided not to shave.

One of the inmates had been in the hole a long time. He told me, "If a guy goes out of here unshaven, he always ends up coming back with more time, and then he never gets out until he shaves." So, reluctantly, I shaved. "Ouch!" They were the dullest blades I'd ever used. When the guard came for me I was embarrassed. I could remember seeing guys released from the hole, and because of the lack of sunlight they always seemed so white till they stood out like a sore thumb.

This court didn't seem much different than the previous one. Besides Captain Herder, the Deputy Warden was there, perhaps because he wanted to see the guy that refused to work on the gas chamber.

"Lewis, are you ready to work on the gas chamber now?" Herder asked.

"I can't do that," I told him firmly, standing my ground. Threatened with more time in the hole, I still refused to budge from my position. To my surprise, Herder responded differently than I thought he would. "I respect you for standing up for what you believe in, Lewis," he said. "I've seen very few men stand up for principles here." I was then released to return to my cell.

Prison discipline was waning at the time. It was a time of construction and transition, as the old was being replaced with the new. I was one of the last men to move out of B Block, its "pruno" caches never discovered. The secret hiding places died with the demolition.

It was an experience in itself to witness the death of an era; in this case, an era in prison reform, from the primitive to the modern. I was part of that transition, and soon found myself in a modern cell block with a toilet and a decent mattress. Even though B Block was demolished long ago, the memories live on in the minds of the unfortunate individuals who were housed there. In one of my recurring dreams, I'm living out my sentence in B Block. It's an unsanitary atmosphere, filled with ugly scenes, like eight or ten guys high on pruno on a Saturday night, waiting in line for their turn outside Mr. Knot's cell. He was sentenced to prison for homosexuality, since it was against the law in the fifties. I always suspected the state of Oregon's consenting adult statute was passed by the legislature for the purpose of legalizing iniquities at the state capitol. This statute made homosexuality legal in the mid-seventies. In a conversation I had with Mr. Knot, he said prison was the best thing that ever happened to him. I always suspected that he worked towards not getting a parole, when his parole date would come up. On the other hand, he indicated that he would rather be involved in homosexual activity on the streets than in prison.

In my dream, I never knew my release date, but was sure the day had passed, and they had forgotten about me. I always tried to get to the administration office to inform them about it, but for some reason, I could never make it. Upon awaking, my body would be totally drained from the anxieties brought on by my dreams. I slowly began to realize I was at home in my own bedroom, and B Block was forty years in the past, dismantled long ago.

Around Christmas time I was moved to D Block. We were allowed to receive a present as long as it didn't weigh more than five pounds, so I took advantage of the holiday and told my mother in a letter that I would like to have five pounds of cashews. By the time they got to me, there was less than three pounds left, but I felt fortunate that the guards and mail handlers would leave that much for me. I was so hungry for "goodies" from the outside, that I overindulged, and developed a severe case of Montezuma's Revenge.

Back in B Block we had taken showers in the laundry room, where up to forty men showered at the same time. For the first five months in prison, I was able to indulge once a week, and was relieved to have access to the small shower at the back of the cell block where there were only four shower heads. It was semi-private, and we didn't have to worry about the lifers ogling us younger guys, uttering x-rated obscenities. "C'mon, baby, drop your soap!" they would say, lustfully, along with other suggestive comments. In their eyes we were considered girls, and this is how they treated us, whistling, making lewd suggestions, and so on. Perhaps the reader could identify with this by imagining how it would feel for a young girl to shower with forty adult male convicts. This is the way I felt, since I was viewed as a female in this environment because of my young age.

Soon after moving into my new quarters, the door slid open for shower line, so I quickly grabbed my soap and towel, eager to experience a feeling of the easier life. No more primitive ways for me! For the first time, without the stress and intimidation, I could enjoy a long, refreshing shower! With anticipation, I stepped into the stall, looking forward to feeling the soothing spray of refreshing warm water on my body. However, I was shocked and horrified by the sight that greeted me! Lying on the floor of the stall was one of the guys, a stream of his life's blood trailing sickeningly through the running water. It disappeared out of sight as it was sucked down the drain into the sewer. He had been stabbed, probably unable to pay a debt consisting of a couple of packs of cigarettes, which are common currency in prison. I never took another shower for the remaining twenty-two months of my prison term. I either took a spit bath in my cell, using cold water, or else I just plain stank.

We had it a lot better in D Block, but there were those who must have been gone from the primitive section too long, since they had forgotten how bad living conditions were in the past, and never seemed to appreciate what they had. They felt they should try to better their circumstances, and this was the surface cause of a strike that followed. A segment of the prison population wanted a strike, not only for humanitarian reasons, but also for the opportunities a strike could present. During the distracting commotion of a strike, the canteen could be robbed, drugs could be stolen from the hospital, or a rival could be eliminated, just to name a few benefits.

Thinking back on the incident, I believe there was a master plan behind the strike. However, the visible issue appeared to be the need for clean socks, bed sheets or higher pay for prison labor. The strike began in the recreation yard, which the warden was obviously in favor of. It was sanctioned by the administration, as well as by the general inmate population. The staff had certain new rules and plans to put into effect in the name of transition, so a strike seemed good for all concerned.

We were allowed to take over the mess hall and the hospital, which was in part, a three-story building. The warden made the statement that we couldn't hold the prison for twenty-four hours, and I remember the cheers from the convicts when the number of hours had passed. We had fallen into the plan of the administration. When the end of convict control came, the building was barraged with tear gas, shot through barred windows. It filled the structure with clouds of the stuff, which devastated our eyes and asphyxiated us, making it impossible to breathe. We had no choice but to vacate the building as the grenades exploded all around us, shrapnel flying everywhere! The administration triumphed with an easy victory, but the strike had to appear real, so it would be necessary for the news media to believe that it lasted for three more days.

It had been a long, sleepless night, and already, I found myself wishing I was back in my cell on a good mattress, even if it did lay on a steel slab. However, we retreated into the baseball field, sprinting from the mess hall to the old laundry building that had housed the shower when B Block existed. The distance was the width of a two-lane city street, and guards on the wall were firing live 30-30 ammo indiscriminately into the retreating convicts, wounding several of the men. Then it came my turn to cross the street. When I was in junior high, I placed first in the fifty-yard dash, and second in the hundred. The sprinting distance in this instance was only a few yards, but it took me half an hour to get across. At least, that's how long it seemed. There were bullets whizzing between my legs, making the careening sounds of a television spectacular. Soon the cracking and hissing of rifle fire was behind me and I stood in the safety of the laundry building, checking to see if I was still in one piece, trying to figure out just what had slowed me down. I wondered if maybe it could be because I smoked. I swore to quit when all this was over. I ran into the boiler room and yelled to the operator, who had been my cell-mate in the hole, "Roger, turn the valves so the whole damned place'll blow!" He had good sense for being only fifteen and behind the walls, or else he'd just plain had his fill of the hole, because the boiler room stayed intact.

The laundry room was another story. It was a wooden structure, destined to be torn down in the near future, and had been torched by ether bombs, a type of Molotov cocktail made from stolen hospital supplies. I threw one of the bombs, and the explosions were gigantic! Smoke from the burning facility could be seen for miles. There was no attempt to bring in firefighters, which led me to believe that the administration had manufactured the strike, and had calculated the loss of the laundry building. This negated the need for a burning permit, and the laundry building was not rebuilt.

We crossed a bridge where Shit Creek ran through the recreation yard, then went to the main compound, where we spent the next three days. Food and water were withheld for that period of time. As far as the outside knew, we were still on strike, although it was actually over after the first day. The administration was pleased to have us under control, locked down in the main yard with armed guards on the wall, giving the appearance to the news media that the strike was still on. The days were hot and the nights cold. We had expected to return to our cells, but the administration had other plans. Thinking we would be going in the next day, I burned my shoes in a bonfire the first night in order to keep warm. The next day, while it was hot, I took off my shirt and never found it again. So I spent some cold, miserable nights out there, with very little sleep.

Water to the yard was shut off, except to a toilet, fully visible to observers on the wall, including lady journalists. I felt a great deal of anger toward such a system that denied a man his privacy to such an extent. Some of the men, in desperation, drank water from the toilet bowl! I could remember how I scolded my dog when I caught him drinking from the toilet, and now I was watching men doing the same thing. I simply could not bring myself to drink out of that toilet bowl, at least not yet! I had found that by arising early in the morning I could lick the dew from various pipes and exercise equipment in the yard and also eat the moist grass, so it helped to quench my thirst some. However, It wasn't nearly enough liquid to keep a body from dehydrating, so how could I be sure that tomorrow I might not be drinking from the toilet bowl also?

With cracked, parched lips and our throats bone-dry, we decided to dig up a water pipe that we figured was buried about six feet deep. The guards allowed the digging for half an hour or so, then realizing we were close to reaching our goal, they opened fire from the wall, with no concern for our safety. About fifteen of us who were in on it, hit the dirt pronto, dodging bullets in the process. Volleys were fired between a guy named Hershey and me, when we were only two feet apart! It's a miracle we weren't hit.

Some of the guards had been nothing more than box boys in supermarkets prior to prison employment. Generally, prison guard applicants wanted to be policemen, but never made the grade, so they applied for the lowest form of law enforcement in the state, and became prison guards. They desired the authority that came with the gun and the badge, because they needed something to elevate their self-esteem. I believe a psychiatrist would say that guard duty filled the vacant spot in their lives, because they were able to push their fellow man around, showing their authority in an abusive way. Turnover was so high that some guards dressed in civilian clothes with just a hat on to indicate their position. They didn't stay on the job long enough to bother with getting a uniform. There were cases where convicts put on a guard hat and simply walked out of the prison during an escape. All this was going through my mind as the careening bullets continued to strike only inches away from me.

Soon the shooting stopped and we started vacating the area, but it immediately started up again, so we laid there in the hot sun, beginning to weaken from hunger and thirst, waiting for their game to end. If you would like to experience what this was like...try going without food and water for three days and nights! We decided to try leaving the area, cautiously...one by one, and it worked. We were able to slowly mingle with the other convicts, becoming inconspicuous, no longer targets.

On the third day, the Catholic chaplain told us, "If you'll surrender the persons responsible for the strike, I'll see to it that you have food and water within the hour." Half an hour later, twelve names were called out on the loud speaker, commonly referred to as the "bitch box." The staff undoubtedly resorted to the "shit list," chose twelve names and called them out over the speaker. Those who were called went in without protest. I would have done the same if my name had been called, because the general population was under siege. I could see the twelve walking in the direction of the hole, knowing that some would not see the light of day again until their bodies were as white as an albino.

Later in the day we were fed some soup, and toward evening we went to our cells, where we had a bologna sandwich. It was several days before things returned to a near-normal routine, but it was never quite the same after the strike. It was obvious that prison conditions were no longer waning.

A guy named "Shorty," one of the convicts, who worked in the prison library, was pushing his delivery cart, slowly making his way up the first tier of D block. Arriving at cell number 7, he announced, "Here's your book, Billy, "The Rise and Fall of the Roman Empire."

"Good deal, Shorty, thanks," Billy Fritz responded. Concealed beneath the book was a hammer and chisel neatly taped together. As soon as it was feasible, Fritz wasted no time in making a hole in the concrete floor of his cell, making preparations to tunnel out. Each time he finished working on the project, he replaced the section of floor he had removed with a gray piece of plywood, which looked exactly like the rest of the floor. A bicycle tire pump that belonged to one of his friends, was used to pump air down to him while he worked in the tunnel. He had to dig under D Block, below an open space, then under E Block, and under another open space, then below the wall and far enough to safely clear it.

What to do with the dirt seemed to be his biggest problem, which slowed down the project considerably. He had me help him carry dirt out to the yard and dump it. We did this by cutting holes in our pockets, and tying a string around the bottom with a bow knot, then filling the pockets with dirt. Afterwards, we went through the checkpoint, where we were patted down, then to the yard where we raised our arms as if we were stretching. Then the bow would come untied, allowing the dirt to trickle down our legs onto the ground as we walked nonchalantly, talking to each other.

Previous attempts to flush it down the toilet were unsuccessful, because dirty water backed up in the other toilets, giving Billy away. That's when I first caught on to what he was up to.

"Hey, Billy, something's wrong with the plumbing up here," I yelled. "When I flush the toilet, muddy water backs up in it!" Sticking his dirty face up out of the tunnel, he replied. "Oh, my god, is it that bad? Get down here, Louie. I want to talk to you!" At the next yard line, I went to see him. "What's the deal, Billy? Where's it coming from?" I asked.

"I'm making a tunnel," he said, "Come on, I'll show you."

"How the hell did you make it through the concrete?" I asked him.

"Well, you remember that night everyone was banging their tin cups against the bars for a couple of hours to get a guard's attention so they could get a doctor to cell 103? That's when I chiseled the hole," he said. I calculated that by the time he was under D Block, about an eighth of his way to freedom, his sentence would be up. The remarkable thing about this project, was that my friend was only doing a two-year stretch. One day the guards caught on and exposed his act. They filled up the hole with concrete, but it was such an ingenious plan, that they didn't do much to him in the way of punishment. He had merely dug a hole, and was not charged with attempted escape.

I had another friend, a twenty-year-old named Stubblefield, who also had an escape plan. He was doing two years for stealing a car, and he simply wasn't made for prison life. He felt that the community trough where prisoners sat defecating in full view may be his opportunity. Water gushed through an eighteen-inch pipe, which carried it to the main sewer. There was a manhole cover over a break in the line that was used for maintenance. Stubblefield figured he could enter this pipe at the break, holding a basketball in front of him, and the gushing water would carry him to freedom by way of the main sewer line outside the prison walls. He told us to call Frenchy, the guard, if the water started backing up. Then he said, simply, "I'm getting out today!" We all looked at him wistfully as he climbed into the hole, knowing that he was determined to get out one way or the other. In our eyes he was already considered a dead man, since we knew how slim his chances were of getting out in such a manner. As the water began backing up very rapidly, we knew Stubblefield was already a free man. He was dead!

"Frenchy, Frenchy, come quick!" I yelled. He was a red-faced, heavy-set man in his fifties, who came running when I called him. "Stubblefield went down that hole!" I told him. Frenchy, seeing the water backing up, knew it was hopeless and started to cry. Pulling himself together, he began running to the control room, possibly the first time he'd run in years. It probably would have been less agonizing for Stubblefield if he had shot himself in the brain. But he chose to go in pursuit of freedom, no matter how short-lived, the end result of a plan born of desperation! His last thoughts were probably of going to the bar that was visible as we sometimes stood wistfully on the top tier watching a red neon light flicker on and off in the distance. After the escape whistle had blown, and we were locked down in our cells, the count began.

Stubblefield was missing! I sat in my cell wondering how in hell justice could prevail in a system like this. Here a young man, someone's beloved child, had been sentenced to death for joyriding in a stolen car.

Almost a year had passed since I was moved to D Block, and it was time to apply for parole, as I had served a third of my time. But I was turned down because I was only nineteen, and the board felt I was still too immature to comply with all the requirements that would be involved. The common prison term was that I would not be able to "live down a parole."

In the meantime, the gas chamber had been almost completed. I watched the construction from the fifth tier, where so many suicides and homicides had taken place when the victims plummeted to the concrete, fifty feet below. Once while I was on the fifth tier, a "goon squad" of five Indians almost made a victim of me, but Verle, a friend of mine, intervened, and the two of us prevailed.

"What's going on up here?" Verle yelled. Sizing up the situation, he could see that it was critical. The Indians were ganging up on me, ready for the kill. "I'll take these three, and you take those two!" he shouted. Somehow, that shook them up so that they surprisingly, turned tail and ran.

The gas chamber was of special interest to me because of my investment in it when I was sent to the hole. Near its completion, I watched as the same crane that dug up my friend, Stubblefield, raised the gas capsule from the dismantled green building and placed it in the newly-constructed gas chamber at one end of the segregation building. With the capsule in place and the roof finished, I took time off from school to make a trip through the checkpoints to the unfinished segregation building, where I walked through the steel door to the gas chamber. Only at this particular time during construction, could this be done. The same guys that urged me not to go to the hole, were putting a finish on the concrete walls, and the glass capsule was already in place.

"Hey, you guys, I want to try out the gas chamber!" I told them, boldly.

"Are you crazy, man? You can't do that!" they pleaded. But remembering my friend, Stubblefield, and how he felt he had to do something he was destined to do, I, too, had to do what my destiny called for. Reluctantly, my friends opened the door to the chamber and placed me in the chair, where Long had so recently sat. Then they strapped me in, hesitated for a moment, then closed the door, screwing it down tightly. Looking through the glass, I saw their grim faces, peering in at me. This was not a joke, and none of my friends were laughing. This was for real! They were witnessing firsthand a man sitting in the gas chamber. But I was seeing it from another viewpoint, that of a condemned man. I began perspiring, and soon found myself hyperventilating because of the lack of oxygen. One of my friends gave the nod, and the door was opened.

"For God's sake, Louie, get out of there before a guard comes!" he pleaded. My straps were loosened, and I became perhaps the only man in the state of Oregon ever to be strapped in the chair inside the gas chamber and walk out alive! I was none the worse for wear, except that I had developed a terrible case of claustrophobia, which has plagued me to this day.

By May, I had moved into the newly-opened E Block, where death row would be housed on the bottom tier until completion of the segregation building. My cell was on the second tier directly above the cells of the condemned. Most of the short-termers, like myself, would move into this newly-constructed block right above death row. I could see those miserable souls, two at a time, walking repeatedly up and down the first tier in front of my cell, during their exercise period. The night two men were to be executed for the same crime, I looked in the windows where it served as a mirror at night and I could see clearly into the cells of the condemned. Just before midnight, the guards came for them, and I could hear unwelcome voices murmuring below me. I could make out only one of the names of the two men.

"Ready, Stark?" one of the guards asked, as the cell doors rolled open. The prisoners reluctantly left, walking the last mile on the way to the gas chamber. Soon their footsteps fell silent, and only the echo remained. Sitting there on my bunk, thoughts of my day in the chamber flashed through my mind! It was an eerie feeling and it would be a sleepless night for me.

On July 19, 1954, I fell out for work line. I hadn't told anyone it was my release date, so I went to work just like every other morning. I didn't want this day marred by anything untimely. As I walked the line through the control room, I fell out and sat down on a bench.

"Louie, get back in line!" the guys begged. "You'll go to the hole again!"

"All right, Louie, get back in line or you're going to the hole," said Lieutenant Cupp, who later became a long-term warden in the prison.

"Wanna bet?" I asked, tauntingly.

Cupp looked puzzled for a second. "You wouldn't do anything like this," he said, hesitantly. "It's your release day, isn't it?" I nodded.

He told me to stay seated and walked over to the control center to make sure it was true. Then he returned, telling me to remain seated, until they processed me. As I sat there, waiting, I could see the door that led to freedom. I had seen this door open for others occasionally, but today it would open for me! Soon I was escorted by a guard to the front office, where my stepdad was waiting. He came up and put his arm around my shoulder, but the overbearing guard suddenly shoved him away, snapping, "He's still a prisoner. Get away from him!"

Even though I was still being treated with contempt, I was beginning not to feel as much like an animal, because now I was about to see the light of day. I was handed some loose-fitting garments, which I hurriedly put on, then the guard walked me out to where my mother was waiting in the car.

"I can tell by the way a convict walks to the car whether he'll return or not," he snarled. "This one will return," he said, with a smirk on his face.

"Not to this prison!" my mother replied, defiantly, ready to come to blows with the arrogant guard. I think she despised him as much as I did.

(See 1950 Pardon, Appendix 1.)

After cashing a twenty-five dollar check at a local bank, we headed for Washington state. My folks were in the process of relocating from California, and they made the move at just the right time to coincide with my prison release. I was certain I wouldn't end up back in prison, as Oregon's rehabilitation system had left a bitter taste in my mouth. The recidivism rate was high, and I could have become a hardened criminal as a result of my experience, but I was determined not to bite off my nose to spite my face!

After my release, I lived on the brink of abiding by the law, and for a time I enjoyed being mischievous. Most of my friends, old and new, didn't like the cops, and neither did I! However, I learned in time, to make room for the establishment and to adapt somewhat. About a year later I went to a Masonic ball where they pledged allegiance to the flag, but I just couldn't bring myself to participate. People stared at me oddly as I just stood there. I remember going to a football game with a girl when I was stationed at Seward Air Force base, a troop carrier wing near Nashville. They played the national anthem and I saluted the flag because I was in uniform. I pledged the allegiance because I was all red, white and blue. But after I viewed the flag through prison bars, it lost its value to me. I was bitter and through with patriotism, yet I still had a desire to serve in some capacity, although not necessarily for this country.

In 1955 I went to Canada and took out landed immigrants' papers, then went to an army recruiting station to join the Canadian Army. They sent me to the Vancouver Barracks, an army post where I stayed several days and took tests for entry. I passed the tests, but wasn't accepted. The Canadian Army wasn't like the United States Army, where once you joined, you were in for the duration. It was like a job. If you didn't like it you could leave, just like quitting a job. They reasoned that since I was an American, I would get homesick and leave. Their approval withheld, I later went to Calgary, where I lived a few months while working in a meat market.

When winter came, it was bitterly cold and mini-skirts were popular. I saw girls in the streets in forty-below weather, bundled up in short winter coats, their upper parts encased in warmth, but naked from the waist down, since that was the days before pantyhose came on the scene. With a quizzical expression, I asked a long-time resident, "How the hell do they manage to keep from freezing?" He replied, matter-of-factly, "Don't you know? They have built-in heaters." In all the sights I've seen in my life, this is one thing that really stands out in my memory, and I'm sure it had something to do with the Women's Liberation movement.

After returning to the States I operated four restaurants and worked in the meat industry from Canada to Mexico. In the meantime I got married and had two daughters, Robin and Whitney. After a short time my marriage failed, and I lived on the left edge of the society I was a part of, like a high-class bum, not excelling at anything. I tried my hand at night-club entertainment and then ended up in the cattle business with a Mexican named Salvador Mesa. Sal had a wife and a live-in girlfriend, which may be the reason why the business failed. I don't know who was to blame for the failure, but I'm certain that the two women didn't help the situation any. It was nearly impossible for Sal to keep the business and the women straight at the same time. It wasn't long until our checks started bouncing, and I was arrested for passing bad checks. After bailing myself out, I skipped town and became a fugitive from justice, along with Sal and the two women.

Then the four of us took what company money that was available, and went to Salt Lake City, Utah. It wasn't long before they began writing bum checks there also, and they seemed bent on a life of crime. At that point I decided to part company with Salvador Mesa.

Looking back on that period of my life, I shake my head at some of the shady deals we made, and the financial scrapes we were involved in. It's no wonder I developed an ulcer that would plague me for many years to come!

FORT WORTH ENCOUNTERS

CHAPTER III

In order to understand Lee Harvey Oswald, you need to understand Ron Lewis or Ron Larson, which was my alias at the time I knew Lee. We were very good friends, and much alike in many respects. However, we differed enough to bring the understanding of Oswald to the fore.

As alluded to previously, I had been in an unsuccessful business venture and had violated the law. After bailing myself out of jail, I jumped bail and became a fugitive from justice. I left Oregon in April 1962, and went underground. The statute of limitations expired in three years, but because of my involvement in the assassination, I hid out for over ten years. Lee Oswald was making preparations to leave Russia just about the time I left Oregon. He had defected to Russia and spent two-and-a-half years there, where he married a girl named Marina. For some reason, he decided to return to America with Fort Worth, Texas, as his destination, which incidentally is where I was headed also.

I chose Fort Worth because in 1956 I met a girl named Bobie, who had moved there from Oklahoma after she graduated from high school. She told me all about the city, how friendly the people were, etc., which I later found to be true.

I left my car and office equipment in Salt Lake City and caught a bus to Fort Worth. Upon my arrival, I walked around town and soon found a small apartment and a job at Hill's Supermarket under the name of Kenneth E. Mason, Social Security Number 528-62-2558. Other than having an assumed name, I lived as normal as I ever did. I was twenty-nine, single, and had friends from various walks of life. One of them was Lee Harvey Oswald. My circle of friends socialized at a level that might be compared to the second rung of the social ladder, yet acceptable people in any society.

I had several friends in Fort Worth. They weren't "good for nothings" nor hippies, yet they weren't model citizens, either. One friend, Stone, was an advertising agent, whose hometown was Evansville, Indiana, where we eventually parted company. His first name as I recall, was Butch, but he was commonly called only by his last name. Stone claimed he was twenty-one, but he appeared older. While doing research for the movie "JFK," Larry Howard told me that Oliver Stone had a friend named Butch Stone, who was twenty-one in 1963, and had been a photographer in Fort Worth. But he advised me to tell

Oliver that Stone wasn't his relative, but was just a guy named Stone. When I told Oliver about Stone, he asked, "Who's that, my long-lost uncle?" Larry and I answered simultaneously, "No, just a guy named Stone." Later, I was able to locate his out-of-state address and phone number, so I called the number. A woman answered, and said he had moved just a couple of months previously. Her voice seemed to contain a note of irritation.

Another friend was named Jimmy Stuart, the same as the movie actor, but his last name was not spelled the same. He was a photographer for Wallace Studios, and I accompanied him to Dallas several times to a music hall, where such musicals as "The Sound of Music," were playing. Jimmy took photos of different couples, after which I would hand them a card with a number on it, and an address where they could purchase the photo. We would then go back to Fort Worth to the studio and develop the film until the wee hours of the morning. But I always managed to get to my regular job at the meat market on time for work.

Jimmy formerly worked as a photographer at Jack Ruby's Carousel Club, taking pictures of individuals and couples, giving them a number so they could purchase the photos at Wallace Studios. However, he found The Music Hall to be more profitable, so he spent most of his time there.

My circle of friends included a married couple, Floyd and his young wife, Nelva Jean, who was only sixteen. Somehow I can't recall their last name, but it seems like it ended with "inski" or "insky." Nelva and I made music together in the local bars. I played the guitar and she played the fiddle, and she always chose the key of "F" to play in, which hindered my singing ability. I first learned of Jack Ruby through this couple.

Nelva Jean had a friend named Karen Carlin. Floyd had been on selling trips with her husband, Bruce, who worked for Jack Ruby. They sold drug store items, which included razor blades that were acquired by hijacking a truck somewhere back East. This was common knowledge among my friends. I figured Ruby was in a sleazy business, and it would pay me to steer clear of him. He was a topic of conversation within my circle of friends, and this provided me with enough insight to sense the mental makeup of the man.

Floyd and Nelva Jean were frequent guests at my apartment, and it was not uncommon for her to visit me while Floyd and Bruce were out of town on selling trips for Ruby. Floyd used the term "riding shotgun" to refer to his work on those trips. He was officially unemployed, and was receiving compensation. Many of my friends received unemployment checks and would also hold some type of under-the-table job at the same time. I remember loaning Floyd money occasionally, to help take care of his wife and new baby. Floyd was not a full-time employee of Ruby, since he only went with Bruce when Jerry Bunker, Bruce's regular helper, was not able to go on the selling trips.

As I mentioned earlier, Nelva was a friend of Karen Carlin, Bruce's wife, so she was a frequent guest at Karen's Fort Worth home. It was being used as a house of prostitution, which was common knowledge to all my friends. Once I went to Karen's house to pick up Nelva Jean. She told me she had gone there to drink coffee and smoke cigarettes, which I never questioned because we were very close friends, and I wanted it to stay that way.

Nelva knew I was a fugitive from justice and she wasn't shy about reminding me of it when she wanted things to go her way. "I'll tell," she'd say, using a subtle form of blackmail. When her husband was out of town on selling trips, Nelva could always be found either at Karen's house or at my apartment, without exception.

Nelva thought the stage names of the strippers were cute, and referred to Karen as "Little Lynn." Nelva was a cute girl, but admitted that she wasn't stripper material, although she was fascinated by those in the profession. Karen would often bring her over to my apartment, where she had access to a telephone, television and good food. Once when she came over, she had been to Jack Ruby's Carousel Club.

"Karen took me to the amateur events at the Carousel Club last night," Nelva Jean told me.

"Did you like 'em?" I asked.

"Yeah," she answered, "I helped her with her routine all week; it was really a fun night. Jack Ruby himself gave me a drink, and he called me Karen's 'little girl.'" Nelva Jean appeared young, innocent and inexperienced, so it was easy to see why Ruby would refer to her as a little girl.

"Wanna' work for me someday when you're old enough?" Ruby had asked.

"Lemme think about it, Jack," she'd answered. Later, she told me, "I think I'd be scared to death to do something like that."

When Karen began working steady for Ruby in 1963, it would be natural to assume he would occasionally ask her about Nelva. "How's my little girl?" he would ask. "Remember, I got dibs on her." If the assassination hadn't taken place, perhaps she would have eventually been one of Ruby's girls. In fact, minutes before Ruby shot Lee, his last words to Karen on the telephone were, "Take care of my little girl." He was referring to Nelva Jean. It seems that I appeared to Nelva as an intellectual, or perhaps someone of a higher stature than others she normally ran around with, and it was with pride that she'd introduced me to Karen. I always had hopes of seeing Karen without Nelva around, but I never said anything about it, and hardly mentioned her except in casual conversation.

Floyd carried a pistol, and wasn't bashful about displaying it. In fact, once when I was in serious trouble with a neighbor because I'd blocked his driveway with my car, Floyd came to my rescue with his pistol. The neighbor was threatening me with a hammer, and had me backed up against the wall of the porch. Floyd had no choice but to come out with the pistol, since I was about to go down. Seeing the pistol, I begged Floyd, "Don't shoot him, don't shoot him! It'll bring the police!" Fortunately, the neighbor backed down, and left.

Karen was just getting started as a stripper, and was a little nervous about it. When I knew her, she worked for a club I thought was called the Cellar Door, and prior to that, she worked part-time for Ruby at the Carousel Club in Dallas, attending the amateur night productions. It is my understanding that Karen eventually worked full-time for Ruby at the Carousel Club in late 1962 or early 1963. Incidentally, while doing research for this book, I discovered that the club Karen worked for was Pat Kirkwood's Cellar in Forth Worth, instead of The Cellar Door.

I met Bruce and Jerry one night, when Stone and I were out joyriding in a 1946 Buick. They were in a 1955 Chevy station wagon. We played a game called "Cat and Mouse," where we would pull into a service station, then the wagon would overtake us, and one of us would be handcuffed in front of the attendant. The tape recorder was playing a police role to make it appear authentic. It was supposed to be all in fun, but I wondered if in reality, it was something else. Perhaps we were unknowingly practicing CIA techniques. I still think it was all in fun, but it is significant that Bruce Carlin and Jerry Bunker were involved in this game, and would later be scrutinized by the Warren Commission in the death of President Kennedy. The recorder belonged to Stone, and he and I used it on another occasion while having fun with two girls in a downtown Fort Worth cafe.

I stayed in Fort Worth only four or five months, but I look back on it with fond memories, and wouldn't have missed it for anything. I could relate many events that would make good reading, but that is not the essence of this book. However, I want to point to my circle of good friends in Fort Worth, because I will later relate to my lack of friends in New Orleans as an incentive for my undivided friendship with Lee Harvey Oswald.

On one occasion, I went on vacation to Corpus Christi, Texas, with a young friend named Rick. He was only sixteen, and I remember getting written permission from his mother to take him with me. I used to get a kick out of Rick, as he was always kidding me about my 1958 Chevy. "There's not a thing wrong with your car," he would tell me, kiddingly. "The only thing it needs is a change of ownership." He would smile, teasingly, indicating that he should be the owner.

As always, I wasn't long on money, so real vacations weren't a part of my life. While in Corpus Christi I worked for the Sam Kane Packing Company as a beef boner, where I met the owner, Sam Kane, who had a multi-million dollar business. He had steel-gray, penetrating eyes, a shock of graying hair, and was built like a football quarterback, seemingly without any flaws. He was a very good-looking man for his age. His outgoing and personable manner, along with his professional appearance, all contributed to his success. It wasn't easy for Kane to open up to people, but we had an instant rapport, so he and I talked on a personal level, a rare experience that I would once again have with Lee.

After spending a short time in nearby Galveston, where we rummaged around docks and fishing boats, Rick and I returned to Fort Worth, where I worked in the meat department of an A.L. Davis Food Market. While in Fort Worth, I became an avid reader of the newspaper, especially accounts of Lee Harvey Oswald's return to America from Soviet Russia. It was, indeed, an interesting and exciting national event that was happening right before me. The newspaper accounts were critical of Oswald, with headlines such as "The Turncoat Returns." I read of a situation in *The Fort Worth Star Telegram*, that lured me to his defense. It told about his Marine Corps discharge being downgraded from honorable to undesirable. I protested that it was unethical on the part of the Navy to take the downgrade action after the fact. I felt that once a person was discharged, that should be the end of it, and to the best of my knowledge, the Marines had a reputation for hitting above the belt, although this time they delivered a low blow.

One day I drove to the Leslie Welding Company where Lee worked. I had no desire to talk to him, but felt sympathy for him because I thought he was being treated unjustly. I drove a black 1958 Chevrolet, registered in the name of Kenneth Eugene Mason, my alias. Nelva Jean or some of my Fort Worth associates, like Jimmy Stuart, might have a picture of that car to this very day.

The flaws in patriotism had already been exposed, in my

eyes, so that was no issue with me, but his discharge was, and I found myself defending him before my friends. However, I didn't meet him that day, and I resolved I probably never would. But I was the type that always wanted to be near something notable, perhaps so that I could say I had been there, or that I had tried it. Certainly, I felt very excited about Lee Harvey Oswald's return!

At the time, John Connally, former secretary of the Navy, was running for governor of Texas. Connally's opponent, General Edwin Walker, was a colorful person and a member of the John Birch Society. I can't say that I cared much about the Society, but I loved Connally even less, so I became a supporter of Edwin Walker. I followed the campaign with interest, and was quite verbal among my friends about his exploits. He became a very colorful politician in my eyes.

The lady that lived next door to me had a son who had recently died of a bleeding ulcer in the Fort Worth jail, so she gave me his wardrobe. She had given him very expensive clothing and in an attempt to put them to good use, I made the effort to circulate in a higher atmosphere, and at a different social level than before. In reality, though, this was counterfeit, a forgery of myself. I attended Christian Science lectures, where many well-to-do persons gathered, but I never did desert my friends at the lower end of the social ladder.

My friend, Stone, and I teamed up to advertise for Wallace Studios, a company dealing in portraits. This gave me an opportunity to use the better clothing that I had been given. We would set up in large department stores, displaying various samples of portrait work, offering coupons for sale to the public. Stone was a good promoter, and we made very good money for those days.

In the fall, around October, we went to Dallas to work a few stores, planning to expand to other states up North, wherever Wallace Studios were located. We needed business cards and advertising for our work, and with this in mind, we went to a printing shop called Jaggars-Chiles and Stovall to have some work done before we left Dallas. We were afraid we wouldn't be able to get in because it was after hours, but there was a light on and the attendant let us in. It was about six or six-thirty in the evening, and was just getting dark. We were making preparations to have our advertisement in copy-ready form for the newspaper in Little Rock, the town we would be going to next, so it would save time. The attendant informed us that he couldn't turn money in to the boss for the work we were having done, because it was against the shop's policy to let anyone in after hours. We gave him about five dollars, and He seemed to be honest in telling us that he would turn the money in, except that he was breaking a rule by letting us in after closing, so he couldn't afford to take the chance. Both Stone and I commented on his honesty after we left, since he didn't have to tell us that he wasn't going to turn the money in.

Stone was a very amusing person, and full of wit. Soon he and the attendant were tearing down the government and the established order in their conversation. That was right up my alley, so I joined in. When he opened up and began talking about his trip to Russia, I realized he was Lee Harvey Oswald. It was my conjecture that he had changed jobs, since the last I knew he was working as a welder in Fort Worth. He showed us some intricate work he was doing with identification on a complex photographic machine.

People on the second rung of the social ladder have a way

of recognizing one another, and this is the way it was between Lee and Stone. They developed an instant liking for each other. We talked a little about Lee's discharge, and the fact that he had gotten a bum rap, and we sympathized with him on that issue. He seemed very pleased, bright-eyed and happy that two young Americans were giving him support during a time that he was not well-accepted by people who knew of his defection.

Lee walked with us to the car. When he saw the 1958 Chevrolet Impala, he asked, "Whose car is that?" I told him it was mine, and he said, "I've always wanted a car like that. I liked the '58 model." When the car was new, Lee was in his late teens, and even though it was almost four years old, it still had an impact on him.

Lee tried to get us to stay in Dallas, but we were adamant about going up North for a while. However, he insisted that we come to see him when we got back to Dallas. We promised him that when we got back, we would get in touch with him. "Scout's honor!" said Stone.

While discussing the fact that I was behind in my car payments, Lee said, "I'd be content to have it for only one night; it's just what I need. Be sure to come straight here when you get back to Dallas." We assured him that we would. This particular car made an impression on Lee, for some reason. Stone and I left him standing on the sidewalk, following us with his eyes, as we disappeared out of sight.

We discussed Lee for a while, then turned our attention to the trip North. We had already telephoned ahead to reserve a hotel room in Little Rock before going to the print shop. It was also necessary to have the telephone number and room number of the hotel, so the advertising copy could be made.

The phone number was to appear in the advertisement we were going to place in the newspaper, upon our arrival the following day.

Stone had a reason for handling things in this manner. "We need a clipping from a former newspaper, in order to get the advertisement in the paper in Little Rock," he said. "I've had problems when arriving in new territory. It eliminates a time-consuming procedure, and thanks to Lee, we can go to work immediately as soon as we arrive." This was true, although the article was counterfeit as it had not yet been published, but our credibility wasn't questioned in any way.

From the very start, Stone and I got into a dispute that continued to get worse as we headed north. We had hired some girls to canvas neighborhoods to sell coupons, and he told me, "Don't fraternize with the employees!" However, I enjoyed making a play for the girls, so I frequently broke the rule. This strained our relationship, eventually causing us to part company at his hometown of Evansville, Indiana.

I had been living under the alias of Kenneth Mason, a name I would eventually use exclusively. I used my birth name, Ron Lewis, for about a month or so when I returned to Dallas. My F.I.C.A. records show earnings of $443.80 from the Dallas area for the last quarter of 1962 under that name.

I think it was around November when I got back to Dallas, since I don't believe I'd been gone a whole month. I put a "work wanted" ad in the paper and also did some advertising for Wallace Studios without getting their approval, just for a day or so to make some easy money. I got a phone in the second apartment I rented there, and the best I can recall, it was under my real name, Ron Lewis. I made enough money to buy a car for fifty dollars, and it drove surprisingly well.

I had left my black 1958 Chevrolet in Evansville, where I parted company with Stone. I purchased it in 1962, while working for a market in Fort Worth, probably sometime in June. I wanted to ditch the car because I was behind on payments, and also because I was ready to switch identities.

As I've brought out, Stone and I got acquainted with Lee Oswald in Dallas, and they developed an instant rapport. At this time, I need to explain a little about each of those individuals. They both had a dire need for a friend, although each had his different reasons. Stone needed a companion, while Lee needed someone to monitor and control the process of his operations, and to keep track of offsprings of his mentality, to keep him from going off the deep end. Lee knew he needed a monitor and was constantly on the lookout for such an individual, although it would have been disastrous for him if he and his friend had the same chemistry, where both lacked resistance.

When Stone and I parted company, I left my car with him and took a bus to Dallas. I was aware that his old friends from Evansville didn't have any real affection for him, and Stone was too close to the forest to see the trees. He was unable to determine that they felt no special fondness for him, and that he had to force their attention. They barely even managed a "hello" when they saw him. After a couple of months Stone began to get a true picture of how his old friends felt about him, and was depressed. I'm certain he returned to Dallas in my car to see Lee, the last person who had brought a measure of happiness to him.

As mentioned earlier, Lee had previously expressed an interest in my car. He could drive, although he didn't have a license. It's not difficult to figure out why a black 1958 Chevrolet with a white stripe along the side, was seen by an eyewitness, a certain Walter Coleman, at the attempted Walker shooting.

The sighting took place in a church parking lot adjacent to the Walker house. Coleman stated, "The car door was open and a man was bending over the back seat, as though he was placing something on the floor of the car." (1)

When I was in Fort Worth previously, I followed the Texas governor's campaign. General Edwin Walker was my favorite candidate over Connally. He was a colorful politician, and stands out vividly in my memory to this very day. There was some news about him in the local paper, which included his address. After purchasing a small camera at a hock shop, I drove to his house and took some pictures. I wanted to see his house, and experience the feeling that came from being in the middle of the action around the events that were taking place.

I was astounded in August 1963 when I found out that Lee had taken pictures of the general's house about the same time I had. He had no doubt gotten the address, 4011 Turtle Creek Boulevard, out of the same paper I had taken it from. I can still remember the house, which appeared to be a two-story colonial-style dwelling. I was happy that I was able to experience the feeling firsthand of having been there. Little did I know that in April Lee would take a shot at the General through one of the very windows I had looked through, and that in August he would inform me that he was the assailant.

After the assassination of President Kennedy, I immediately retreated to Harlengen and destroyed the pictures of General Walker's house. They were burning a "hole" in my pocket all the way from New Orleans.

In winter of 1962, I returned to Little Rock and rented an

apartment, obtaining a telephone under my alias, Kenneth Mason. I obtained work in a meat packing plant. It was here that my car was stolen by four men who were wanted by the FBI for bank robbery. They lived in the same apartment building I did, and wanted to borrow my car to give their car a shove, but the only problem was…they didn't bring it back. Being a fugitive, I couldn't take a chance of getting caught by reporting the car missing, so there was nothing I could do. It was only fifty bucks, but that car was my only transportation!

Things weren't going smoothly in Little Rock, and it was evident that the Fort Worth-Dallas encounters were clearly behind me, so I wouldn't return to that area. It stood to reason that I would soon have to think about finding another place to move to.

DETOUR TO NEW ORLEANS

CHAPTER IV

Politics took a back seat with me for the time being, except for attending a George Wallace rally. The funny part is that I don't even remember where it took place. The FBI visited me at my apartment in Little Rock to ask questions about the alleged bank robbers that had been living there. I made the slip that they'd stolen my car and they wondered why I hadn't reported it to the police. I was sure one of them had taken a picture of me, and I had the strong feeling they figured I was a fugitive and were investigating me, so I decided to leave town.

As hard as I tried to be angry at the bank robbers for stealing my car, I never failed to be amused at them. One day they said,

"Let's pool our money and get some bread and bologna." But no one had any money. Later they said, "Let's pool our money and get a bottle." One came up with a quarter and another with twenty cents, and soon they had enough for a bottle of wine. I thought it was very amusing that they chose a bottle over something to eat, when I knew they were famished.

In Little Rock I used the name of Kenneth Mason again, and I'm certain the phone was in that name and that there should be a record of it. After I wiped my fingerprints clean from the apartment, so there would be no evidence left for the FBI, I told my girlfriend "goodbye" and left for Fort Smith.

I made a couple of slip-ups. I left a bottle of whiskey with my fingerprints on it in the refrigerator. Also, Fort Smith, Arkansas was a jumping-off place for people who were trying to evade the law in Little Rock. If fugitives left Little Rock, the FBI would likely assume they went to Fort Smith, so I exercised poor judgement when I chose that town to go to. Also, I had bought some clothing in Little Rock, and left town owing the bill, another point that wasn't exactly in my favor. I arrived in Fort Smith, not realizing that it was merely a detour to New Orleans.

I worked for another packing company in Fort Smith and lived in a boarding house that most single men landed at when arriving in that town. I shared a room with a young guy named Frank. He came home on a Friday evening and said the FBI was at his place of employment looking for me. I didn't know if they knew who I really was, but my statute of limitations hadn't expired yet, and I wasn't about to take any chances! Within minutes we went to the bank, drew out my two-hundred dollars in savings and left town in Frank's car, headed for Mobile, Alabama.

Frank decided he liked Mobile, so he stayed. However, it reminded me of the Fort Smith situation, and I had learned a lesson from that, so I bought a bus ticket to Florida. I'm glad I met Frank, because his name, through word association, enabled me to remember the name of the man who took Lee to Dallas to meet with Maurice Bishop the following year. His name was also Frank.

I worked for a resort hotel during the three weeks I was in Florida. I was concerned about a law that required people who worked in almost any area of employment to get a police clearance card, which of course, I wasn't able to do. I did manage, however, to stall on that point until the close of the tourist season. The police frequently questioned people on the street about their cards. If you didn't have yours, they would give you a chance to get it, and if you didn't come in on the appointed day, they would come to your place of employment to find out why you failed to show up. This doesn't sound like the good old U.S. of A., and I am sure it was a violation of civil rights, but as you will remember, civil rights was in its infancy in the sixties.

When the hotel closed for the season at the end of February, I was offered a job in Maryland by my employer, but declined the offer because I was afraid to stay at one place of employment too long. Instead, I took the bus to Savannah and went to work in a meat market, where my boss got upset with me for calling the black people "Ma'am" and "Sir." I simply could not continue working in an atmosphere like that, nor in any of the other establishments segregationally inclined.

Those were the days of the "freedom riders," so I volunteered to work for the NAACP, and was assigned to a project, joining them in racial demonstrations. My job was to ride the city bus with a group of other Whites, where we would sit in the back, forcing the Negroes to sit in front. This they were reluctant to do, which was a complete surprise since the Blacks were customarily forced to sit in the back, and I thought they would be happy to receive equal treatment. But that wasn't the case. I couldn't understand why these people didn't want to go to the front to exercise their rights. It reminded me of the story of "Homer," that Mary Baker Eddy alluded to in one of her writings. It was a story about a boy who had been in a dark closet all his life and had eaten nothing but burnt bread and water. When the authorities found him and took him into custody, he soon wanted to return to the environment where he felt comfortable…his dark closet where he could get his burnt bread and water.

Over the years, minorities, especially Blacks, have become fairly well adjusted, even though some were reluctant to accept their liberation. Although I wasn't aware of it at the time, my actions would earn me a place in the Banister apparatus and consideration for a job in Clinton, Louisiana, involving the Black registration drive.

While I was in the segregated city of Savannah, I came across a situation that caused me not to take the assassination plot that was developing in New Orleans too seriously. There was sentiment against John Kennedy because of his stand against segregation, and I hardly encountered a person who liked him. While sitting on the porch of the rooming house where I lived one evening, I heard an interesting conversation. There were seven or eight persons involved in a discussion with my landlady, who was sitting in the porch swing, a common sight in Savannah. She was being confronted by a group of neighbors because she had a portrait of the president hanging on her living room wall, a mortal sin in this segregated town in the year 1963. Her name was Emmy Lou Harris, the same as the popular country singer of today, and she was seventy-eight years old. She was being harrassed by the group, who called her a traitor, and was in the process of defending herself.

"If this kinda' thing is allowed to go on by somebody your age, what can we expect from our younguns' who're having integration forced on 'em in school?" they asked.

"I've had a portrait of the president on my wall for the last fifty years," Mrs. Harris responded in her defense. "Y'all have been in my house and know I'm telling the truth, and just because this president is not popular with you, I'm not gonna' break my tradition now." That satisfied those who were present, so she kept her portrait of Kennedy hanging on the wall.

There were people saying they wanted to kill Kennedy because of his stand on segregation, and I became accustomed to hearing threats made against him. This was so common in Savannah that even the authorities were weary of hearing them. I was eventually put in jail over the weekend for racial integration actions and was surprisingly, not fingerprinted. I was arrested under the name of Kenneth Mason, which is likely a matter of record. I think I was charged with disturbing the peace. While I was in jail there were two preachers in the same cell, charged with stealing from the collection box!

Upon my release I went to Chattanooga, Tennessee, where I worked for two meat markets, both run by Jewish people. I believe it was in this town that I attended a George Wallace rally in June 1963. I recall that Wallace was flanked by Alabama state troopers, even though he was outside of Alabama. The speaker said, "There has been both good and bad said about George Wallace, but one thing is for certain, before you stands a brave man." Mr. Wallace looked at the South as the hope for America's free enterprise system. He pointed to dangers in centralized left-wing governments, and said the John Birch Society was better than left-wing groups. He criticized Kennedy for writing an executive order that sent troops to establish a housing regulation

MY APARTMENT AT 1923 IBERVILLE IN NEW ORLEANS.

that Congress wouldn't approve.

Before leaving Savannah, and prior to going to jail for integration activities, I went to Washington, D.C. and on to New York City, which I will elaborate on later. After going to Chattanooga, I went to New Orleans, arriving on or before the middle of July. As soon as I arrived, I walked up Canal Street near the Louisiana State University Medical Center, and rented an apartment on Iberville Street.

The apartment was one half of a small duplex, and as you stand on Iberville between North Roman and North Prieur and face the apartment, you will see the number "1923" on the duplex on the left. It was small, but clean and freshly-painted, but you can see from this photo taken in December 1990 by one of Oliver Stone's production crew workers, that time has taken its toll on the apartment.

When I arrived in a new town, I would obtain a city map so I could become familiar with my surroundings. In New Orleans I highlighted on the map the route from my apartment at 1923

Iberville Street to my work at the Viking Packing Company located at 346 Calliope. I had a temporary job shelling shrimp, and also worked a couple of days helping repair two small fishing boats, while waiting for the job at the packing company to open up. I cannot remember the exact date I started working there, but it was at least by the first of August.

I made frequent trips out to the garbage can, because we had a cockroach problem in the summer of 1963. However, I discontinued going outside at night after Lee told me of shooting at Walker. It was in this apartment that I spent many nights worrying over what Lee was up to, and trying to figure him out.

This was the route I took to work: As I went out my door, I took a left on Iberville and took the first right on North Roman and walked one block to Canal, then caught a bus or a streetcar to Camp Street. After meeting Lee there, I began to get off on Magazine Street, because we would meet every morning or so at the Crescent City Garage. I met Lee on Camp Street, which was my first encounter with him since Dallas. During that first meeting he handed me a "Fair Play for Cuba" leaflet.

It was about 7:30 A.M. when I encountered Lee Oswald in front of 544 Camp Street. I recognized him right away. There were certain characteristics that made him stand out, such as his physique and the way he stood so erect, with his neck protruding forward; just the general features of his profile.

When I first met Lee I was going by the name of Kenneth Mason, and now I was living under the alias of Ron Larson. I was apprehensive about opening up to him, since I wasn't sure how he would react or if he could handle the fact that I was living under an alias. It seemed as if he also had some reservations about me, as he approached me with caution at first. I accepted a "Hands Off Cuba" leaflet from him, after which we spoke for a minute or two, then I went around the corner to LaFayette and dropped the leaflet in a trash can. I wasn't exactly sold on Castro, and I didn't want to become active in Oswald-type politics. However, I was attracted to things of that nature, and as time went on I eventually became involved.

Years later, I suspected Lee had used my car the night he shot at General Walker. I was convinced that the 1958 black Chevy with a white stripe on it that was seen at the Walker shooting, was mine. Although he had no regrets about using my car, it made him a little edgy being around me at first, because he didn't know how I would take it. However, before long the initial uneasiness vanished, and we soon became good friends.

HANDS OFF CUBA LEAFLET. (2)

BANISTER'S RECRUITER

CHAPTER V

My relationship with Lee was that of a friend. I'm not sure what his relationship was with me, but I believe I was his best friend. There are some things I held back from him, such as the fact that I never did tell him I disliked Castro, probably because I didn't want to hurt his feelings. When Castro started shooting people and digging mass graves, I really turned against him. Lee didn't tell me of his Mexico trip in advance, even though he employed me to give Banister reports on the "Gillis Long for governor" campaign. We had an ongoing dialogue for two months during the summer of 1963. I'm going to try to cover every detail because of the gravity of what I am relating. There have been publications that depict those being named as conspirators in the assassination, among other things, but I am one of the few witnesses coming forward to attest to those things.

There was indeed an element of truth in the stories that exist. Lee had an office at 544 Camp Street and this was in a lonely and isolated room upstairs. He soon became bored of his isolation, however, and moved his activities around the corner to Magazine Street in the Crescent City Garage.

Lee was Banister's recruiter and he needed to be in contact with people. The Crescent City Garage served this purpose, as it was in close proximity to Banister's office at 544 Camp Street. Lee's office was moved to the garage, which gave off the odor of tires and oil, and there was sometimes a mechanic milling around, tending to his duties. In fact, this was the garage that serviced cars that belonged to the CIA and various

THE CRESCENT CITY GARAGE IN NEW ORLEANS

other federal agencies. Mr. Alba, the owner, had his office on the left in 1963, but at some point in time it was moved to the right to accommodate a parking facility. Behind this office on the left was what Lee called his office, where we met many times for our morning discussions.

I had no other friends in New Orleans except Lee, and I was pleased whenever I had the opportunity to see a familiar face. Because of my name change, I hoped Lee wouldn't recognize me from our previous encounter, but this was a futile wish. Nonetheless, when we became friends, these things didn't seem to matter. We came to know too much about each other to be divulging any shared secrets.

When Lee and I were conversing the day we met on Camp Street, we talked about the leaflets, among other things. He asked me to step to the outer edge of the sidewalk and compare the number on the leaflet with that on the old Stevedores and Longshoremen's Building that now housed Banister's office. I did as Lee requested and noted that the number 544 matched, and for some reason, this delighted Lee. As I said, I walked around the corner and deposited the leaflet in the trash can, but that act would not end my relationship with Lee. I often wondered if he ever retrieved any of the leaflets that people discarded so he could use them again. I peeked in the can the next time I went by, and the leaflet was gone. I don't imagine that many people were interested in giving fair play to Cuba in those days. Lee didn't hand out those leaflets simply because he was such a devoted communist, but it was partly an excuse to come into contact with young men like myself, so that the select few that Banister was seeking to employ in certain tasks, could be found.

Only someone who had lived in that era, could really ap-

CRESCENT CITY GARAGE INTERIOR OFFICE

As you look at this office, you will see that it's about fifteen or twenty feet long. It is now on the right side of the building whereas in 1963, it was on the left side. So what presently is the front of the office, was then the back.

On the opposite side is what Lee called his office at the time I knew him. It was just behind this office, where there was a cement-covered foundation he called his "chairs," and there were some loose boards above the chairs where he placed his papers.

preciate how brave Lee was to hand out communist literature in 1963. It was a difficult task as communism was very unpopular. About the worst thing one could be called was a communist. It probably would be difficult for the youth of today to focus in on how much of a challenge it was to distribute literature in support of a communist nation, just ninety miles from the American mainland.

I actually handed out a leaflet, but it probably didn't bother me as much as it would have most Americans. At the time, I admired Lee for standing up for what he believed in, or whatever it was that motivated him in the face of such opposition, even though I soon learned this charade was a front for his activities. Lee did attract modest attention. After all, where would most Americans who had been exposed to such television programs as "I was a Communist for the F.B.I.," get the chance to see a real live communist, except right there on Camp Street in New Orleans?

The 544 Camp Street building was indeed intriguing. It reminded me of B block back in prison before it was torn down. The building, constructed of decomposed brick, was long and narrow, like a cell block. It seemed as if it should be connected to a presidential assassination with its shady conspirators, agents and soldiers of fortune in a shabby and antiquated 1800s setting. It was a place where gun-running was legal up until shortly before my arrival. The local authorities had grown accustomed to those activities, and still sanctioned their clandestine behavior.

With Operation Mongoose in full-swing, Banister had become powerful, and he savored the power he would regain by the participation that his former governmental connections would assure him. However, with the president's suspension of Operation Mongoose, his operations became illegal. But he still retained power, and continued efforts against Castro Cuba in spite of the presidential order forbidding it. Local authorities were slow at interpreting the new federal direction that called for halting raids against Cuba. The pin-prick raids against the country by small anti-Castro forces such as Alpha 66, at first backed by the CIA, were later financed by Carlos Marcello. The word "mongoose" refers to a flesh-eating mammal that surrounds its victims, and attacks with a repeated pin-pricking motion. In this particular instance it had reference to underground forces, which in a sense acted much as the literal mongoose; hence the operation was thus named. This makeup provided a perfect cover for the occupants of 544 Camp Street, and would climax in the formulation of a plan to assassinate the president of the United States. I first learned about it during the latter part of August 1963.

The recent Ricky White allegations convey that his father, Roscoe White, shot Kennedy from the "grassy knoll" on orders from the CIA. I can corroborate that statement, inasmuch as I had prior knowledge that the CIA faction I worked for conspired to kill Kennedy. This faction included Jacob Rubenstein, better known as Jack Ruby, Lee Harvey Oswald, David Ferrie and Roscoe White. Guy Banister worked closely with the ONI, so this raises serious questions about a possible involvement.

All the evidence I've been able to gather, points to the fact that the assassination in one way or another was deeply rooted in 544 Camp Street, where Lee and I frequently met and talked. It was a place where ideology had no firm grip, where both the right and the left were housed, and where both segments got along remarkably well without friction. I feel I must bring this out, because I'm not as interested in making sense as I am in relating the events as they happened. Lee told me his uncle had an office in this building, then he told me they weren't really related, that Mr. Banister was a friend of his uncle, and Lee thought of him as a relative. As Lee and I began to form a friendship, the "uncle" dialogue dissolved.

Lee was aware that the CIA was quartered across the street in what I thought was the Federal Building, and he told me Banister worked for the CIA. In fact, he told me just about everything that is written about Banister, as well as the additional things I'll be bringing out.

For the sake of those readers who are unfamiliar with Banister, I would like to describe him to some extent. He was a former FBI agent in charge of the Chicago office until the late fifties, when he retired, taking a deputy chief position with the

New Orleans Police Department. He was fired after pistol-whipping a party at a restaurant. There are some who claim this activity was a front, just an excuse to go underground and work for the CIA.

Banister's working for the CIA is a fact that is indisputable, but the story surrounding his departure from the police department was questionable. As many defeated law officers do, Banister went into the private detective business. His biggest client was the United States government, primarily the CIA and the FBI, two distinctly different agencies. He had worked for the CIA in Operation Mongoose in the Pontchartrain Secret Training Camp project, while buying and distributing arms to Cuban anti-Castro groups. He continued even after the presidential order to disband Operation Mongoose. Because of his refusal to comply, Banister became a big man in the anti-Castro network, still operating under the impression that he was backed by the government.

I remember seeing revolutionary-types coming and going from this building where I met Lee during the summer of 1963. The incoming Cubans mostly wore American combat boots, and some were dressed in civilian clothing with a fatigue hat or field jacket. One or two in the group would wear full combat attire, and they stood out like a sore thumb. David Ferrie would usually load them into dusty pickup trucks or vans and take them to the secret training base, but I never knew of Banister accompanying them. I was told that he never left the office.

One of the jobs Banister contracted from the FBI was to create a file on college students who had left-wing tendencies. Lee had been employed to go on college campuses to distribute left-wing literature, turning over to Banister the names of those expressing an interest. I never did like those activities, because it seemed to me like entrapment, just to build an impressive file for the FBI. Soon Lee was promoted, and at the time I met him in New Orleans, he was recruiting individuals to infiltrate campuses in order to obtain information as well as to engage in other tasks.

This CIA faction was keenly interested in the prevailing governor's race which was ongoing in New Orleans at that time, while Lee was on the lookout for an individual to attend rallies and report on them. He was getting paid for the information he turned over to Banister, because he made the statement, "I get paid for information like this." Although he worked for Banister, he was paid by someone else. I am certain it was the FBI, and that he was paid the sum of two-hundred dollars a month.

As cold war criteria diminished between the Soviets and the free world in the nineties, Soviet intelligence officials raised the lid on a ten-inch thick file on Lee Oswald. It shows that Soviet authorities thought he was a United States agent during his 30-month stay in Russia. This strengthens what Lee said to me, concerning the "Gillis Long rallies; "I get paid for this kind of information." I always knew Lee was a paid FBI informant, but I knew he didn't completely trust his contact. He despised the fact that the FBI and the president weren't on the same track. He once said to me, "It's difficult to deal with people that are not predictable." He even told me the name of his FBI contact who lived in Dallas.

Having been provided diplomatic immunity from local authorities, Banister had a perfect setup for clandestine activities, such as gun-running or whatever, and he could do that under the guise of the CIA or the FBI. Local authorities didn't doubt Banister's credibility until James Garrison began his investigation and put Clay Shaw on trial for conspiring to kill the president, and Banister's activities began to come to light. Shaw was acquitted, probably because people like myself were afraid to come forward to testify.

There is unmistakable evidence that Banister usually acted on orders from higher up, at least from Shaw. I am certain that Shaw was in on the conspiracy to kill the president, because Lee told me this before the act took place, and I saw the conspiracy begin to unfold. Was I supposed to believe that Lee or some other faction killed Kennedy? Nonsense! There is absolutely no way I can buy that. From my personal knowledge and all the evidence to the contrary, this would be too absurd for me to accept.

One of the more dominant persons who worked for Banister was David Ferrie, a very important CIA contract agent. His ties to Banister were beyond being interfered with; in fact, they seemed unbreakable. Elements within the CIA had found him useful, although they took into consideration his ties with Banister. David was Banister's contact with the Pontchartrain base, as well as one of his contacts inside Cuba. David did many jobs for Banister that required an element of secrecy and confidence. Having previously sold arms to Castro, Banister was now selling them to the anti-Castro faction, a business Jack Ruby had been in for quite some time. He had an existing pipeline into Cuba that the Banister apparatus utilized.

Ruby's interests revolved around drugs from China, channeled through Cuba. That's what he had been receiving as payment for delivery of arms. However, I never could understand how or why Chinese drugs would find their way to

Ruby through the anti-Castro elements. No doubt, some double-dealing was involved.

Had Lee been reading too many James Bond novels? Ruby was receiving fringe benefits in the way of drugs behind Banister's back. But how and why from China? This has been a perplexing question for me, because I never learned the answer. I only knew that it kept Ruby in tow. It was something he could turn into money, not caring who got hurt in the process. Little did he know that he would suffer in the end as a result of his clandestine dealings. Castro was an ally of China, and like I said, it has been puzzling to me why China would aid the anti-Castro elements by giving Ruby drugs, especially opium, as a subsidy for delivering arms to China's enemies. Since I've had some time to reflect on it, I think perhaps I have solved the problem, even though it's a James Bond-type solution. No doubt China resolved that the arms would reach the anti-Castro insurgents, regardless of their interference. But why shouldn't they capitalize on their losses, which would likely be calculated in a cold war, by injecting drugs into America's mainstream, polluting those who were eligible for the draft.

Banister utilized Ruby's pipeline to Cuba with some reluctance. But Banister was onto his act, and Ruby may not have known that until shortly before the assassination and Lee's death. Even though Banister was edgy about Ruby's drug problem, he put up with it because Ruby had become a proficient arms buyer. This was where his main value lay in connection with Banister. I cannot put enough emphasis on the importance that Lee placed upon Ruby in the apparatus. I can't recall his exact words, but he implied that Ruby had made enough purchases to merit a near-genius status in the field of arms procurement. I can't speak for other time periods, but in August and September 1963, I had firsthand knowledge that Banister was utilizing Ruby's pipeline.

I had detected some concern expressed over the fact that the Ruby connection had posed a problem for Banister because of the drug deliveries. Ruby's gun-running activities stemmed from the fifties for various clients. He developed the plan to offer his Cuban pipeline to Banister, claiming to be a right-winger and at the same time accepting kickbacks in drugs.

This was distasteful to Banister, but he decided that rather than attempt to work on and try to resolve these existing problems with Ruby, he would use them to his own advantage. He would allow him to accept kickbacks in drugs without his sanction, but would file the knowledge away for future use, so he could be assured of Ruby's allegiance. These are not my own assumptions, but what I learned from my conversations with Lee.

As for David Ferrie, he had been a senior pilot for Eastern Airlines and had dabbled in religion, studying to be a priest. But Ferrie was defrocked for the same reason he lost his position with the airlines. He was a homosexual.

He also had a friend named David Lewis, whom I knew of but had never met. He was also employed by Banister.

Practically everything I learned about David Ferrie was from Lee. Ferrie was forty-six years old and dressed like a clown. It wasn't difficult to recognize him the first time I had a conversation with him. Lee told me not to underestimate David just because he was a homosexual. He could be very dangerous to his opposition and should not be taken for granted, because he was a genius in his field as a soldier of fortune.

Lee said that Ferrie had to believe in his cause, which was fortunate for Lee, because that meant David was predictable to some degree, and it was difficult for him to work with someone who wasn't. He said that as he got to know me better, he hoped he would find that I was also predictable. Of course, Lee didn't stop to relate this to himself, nor even consider the fact that he, himself, was very difficult to predict!

Among other things we discussed was an injury David received in the line of duty. I realize these things are brought out in certain publications, but the reader should find it interesting to learn that Lee confided these facts to me before they ever became public knowledge. They are new revelations in the sense that they originated in the mind of Lee Harvey Oswald, and were told to me directly by Lee himself.

"David was injured while on a CIA flight to a point inside Cuba," Lee said. "He should've received the Purple Heart for that wound, but David's type of soldiering never sees the light of day. He'll never get recognition for it." I discounted the story as being one that David might tell his crony admirers, and at the time I suspected Lee was one of them. Little did I know then that I would read of the flight and the injury in a book called "Betrayal," by Robert Morrow, a few years later. Morrow, incidentally, made the flight with David.

"I can relate to David's situation concerning his wounds," Lee said. "In working for the CIA you never get recognition for them. I have a cut on my left wrist where I had to fake a suicide attempt, and it was in the line of duty."

I examined the cut, but was a little apprehensive about believing him, as I always was with Lee. He was so young and had been involved in so much until I was skeptical about some of the things he was telling me. At the time, I thought the cut on his wrist might have been the result of an accident. It looked as if it were superficial, rather than life-threatening. After I began reading about his life, I found out that what he told me was true, including something he'd said about it being on the periphery of David's wound. He said it was in the line of duty, and that he would never get recognition for it. "Let me tell you a good one, though," Lee said. "I got gonorrhea in the line of duty." Seeing my puzzled expression, he continued. "That's right, Ron," he told me with a grin, "...the only man in the Marine Corps to get gonorrhea in the line of duty, and I didn't get reprimanded for It!"

"How the hell did that happen?" I asked.

He replied, "Getting information from some Japanese prostitutes."

Another person associated with Banister was Clay Shaw, head of the International Trade Mart. Lee and I had talked about him a good deal, which I will refer to later on. My impression was that Shaw was in a position to advise Banister, as well as to come down on him hard when things went wrong. I later relate that Banister gave the orders to carry out the Clinton project on advice from Shaw, so they wouldn't miss out on an opportunity like they missed out on in Jackson, Mississippi. This showed me that Shaw was Banister's superior. Mentioning Shaw prompts me to tell of Lee's demonstration when he handed out leaflets in front of the International Trade Mart that Shaw directed. Lee was assisted by two young men. He later told me, "I didn't demonstrate on my own. It was set up by Shaw, and he called WDSU-TV, to have the demonstration televised." This was something Lee hadn't expected. The incident took place on or about August 16. "The demonstration was part of my job with Banister and Shaw," he said, "and Shaw paid me a bonus." I happened to know it was the sum of ten dollars. When we used the money to buy ice cream cones, he said, "We can thank Clay Shaw for our ice cream today." There can be no doubt about who was behind this incident. Lee was ordered to participate in it, even though some believe he acted on his own. However, I want to assure them that he acted on orders from higher up. To appreciate what the Banister apparatus consisted of, one would have to understand how the CIA is woven together. It would be necessary to know how it evolved, its role in serving the FBI, the government and its right-wing factions.

The CIA evolved into a Cyclopean type of government within a government. In the presidential administrations that preceded Kennedy, there was the need for a branch in which the president had control. But such leaders had distanced themselves from the CIA, so that they didn't have to take responsibility for its many actions. When clandestine operations were necessary, the president would come out clean in the public eye. Agents were then appointed at the top of the branch, while others evolved from the bottom. In time, shadowy and ruthless characters became powerful in the organization, and standards were established at a point where the two forces came together, sometimes clashing in contrast to the initial plan.

By the time Kennedy arrived, control over the branch had been lost. The secretive fragmentation that evolved, developed an agency of little gods with minimal supervision, as it was at 544 Camp Street. Men who had evolved, and were once government-controlled, had taken over a section of a provisional government agency. To stay in business, they needed causes that were in the interest of national security, so they formed the "Anti-Communist League of the Caribbeans" and the "Friends for a Democratic Cuba." To prove that they were an enterprising bunch of people, where ideology kept a low profile, "Fair Play for Cuba" gained their silent consent and found a resting place with them.

These were strange bedfellows, opposing forces resting together, but I didn't give a great deal of thought to that unusual situation at the time it was facing me. However, in the years that followed, especially in view of the subsequent assassination, I gave further thought to the situation. I questioned Lee's connection to such right-wing causes, and why the Banister apparatus would be associated with Lee's left-wing leanings. It became apparent that he was a government agent, regardless of beliefs to the contrary. Even so, he had his own personal political views. "I'm a Marxist," Lee said, and associated this with Great Britain's program on socialized medicine.

I can give a firsthand eyewitness account of most of Lee's activities in New Orleans, from conversations I had with him. I learned that he was acutely aware of Banister's opposing situation, but wanted desperately to be involved in the intrigue that Banister's activities provided. He showed self-control, in the sense that he could live with those activities, even though they expressed right-wing tendencies.

Based on our previous conversations, I had the gut feeling that Lee, at one point, would turn the tables on the Banister apparatus. But the September 7 message from Cuba would shatter any hopes for such an event taking place. For the time being, Lee had fallen in line with the relaxed atmosphere that existed at 544 Camp Street, where ideology was left sleeping. Because of his 007 fantasies, coupled with his fatal obsessions,

GARY OLDMAN PORTRAYING LEE IN "JFK" MOVIE SCENE.

or any other motives that might have attracted him to that location, he was obviously very happy in that environment. It
was inevitable that he would find such a place of international
intrigue, even though it might have compromised his princi-
pals. I couldn't have found him anyplace else, as this situation

77

was tailor-made for Lee Harvey Oswald.

I had gotten a new job and was on my way to work when I met Lee again. This time he wanted to show me his new office. The one he had previously had been upstairs at 544 Camp Street. It didn't serve his purpose as well as it did on the street level where he had access to people. A girl and her boyfriend were using a room next to Lee's upstairs office for a photo processing lab, and that made him feel uncomfortable. Also, it had no air conditioner and it was stifling hot that time of year. "I lost five pounds from sweating in that little room!" he told me. He realized soon after moving in that he needed to relocate, and once this was accomplished, it made it handier for him to recruit and hand out an occasional Fair Play for Cuba leaflet, a means to develop dialogue with young individuals, such as myself. This was a good way to find the needles in the haystack that Banister wanted, and the street-level office in the garage was like a release from confinement.

While taking me to see his office, we went into the indenture on Magazine Street, that turned out to be the Crescent City Garage, complete with the odor of tires and oil. This would be my meeting place with Lee until my last visit with him on October 11, just before the assassination. Behind the office, on the left as you walked in, was a concrete-covered foundation along the wall. Lee, pointing to the structure in an amusing gesture, smiled. "Look, my office has chairs!" he said, and we both laughed. We would spend many hours sitting on that foundation while holding our discussions.

Mr. Alba's office was no more than twenty-feet-long. We would go behind it to Lee's office, where we enjoyed a degree of privacy for our visits. I was a little edgy because I was afraid the garage manager would object, but Lee reassured me. I remember his exact words: "Don't pay any attention to 'em. They're used to me being here."

Behind us, concealed by some loose boards, was Lee's hiding place where he could slip in his hand and get his papers, among other things. He told me he kept certain items there because he was afraid he might be searched while he was out during the day. I looked at him a little strangely because I just couldn't visualize him being into anything so clandestine that the police would be that inquisitive of him. He assured me, however, that they were indeed curious.

After learning about Lee's pistol and rifle I asked him if he kept his pistol in the hiding place. He answered, "Well, sometimes I wear it in Banister's office, but I don't keep it in the hiding place because the doors are usually open, even at night."

"Well, where do you keep it?" I inquired.

"You'll never believe it, Ron," he replied, "I keep it in that damned old squeaky air conditioner in Banister's office. Mr. Alba keeps the tools locked up, and these winos have no use for papers. Most of 'em don't even know how to read or write, and if they found a pistol they would hock it for a bottle of wine. So the papers are safe here. In fact, if you ever need to get a message to me, be sure to put it in the hiding place. I check it for messages every morning." Even though Lee told me I was the only one who knew about it, I was still afraid others might see me use it, putting me in jeopardy. I never trusted Lee's statement that I was the only one who knew about the hiding place. Now, in looking back, I feel that he was right, that I was the only one who had knowledge of it.

I was afraid that others might have had access to this secret place, and I wasn't about to take any chances in being around there at night, due to the possibility of CIA people using it. But Lee was still eager for me to use that method of communication, although I never found it necessary to do so. He was no doubt fulfilling a 007 fantasy, or was he?

At the time, I had no idea he acted out his fantasies, but the passage of time would change many of my beliefs about his capabilities. I had always wanted to check this hiding place, because Lee told me if anything ever happened to him, I should check it for an important message. I was to learn more about what that information might have been, as time passed. But when I went to check the place twenty-seven years later, the wooden wall had been torn down, and the office had been moved to the other side of the garage. I wasn't even able to find the "chairs" that once existed. Evidently the construction workers weren't concerned with any bits of paper that might have been left in the hiding place, so if they came across any, they wouldn't have thought to salvage them. Lee might have left incriminating assassination evidence against Banister, but if he did, that evidence will probably never be found.

Lee told me that a man was being trained to kill the president, and would be positioned in the Dallas police department through the Ruby connections. He didn't say he was a Banister employee, but he did say he had been at Lake Pontchartrain Secret Training Camp, and that his name was Roscoe White. Banister supplied all the men and weapons for the training camp, although the camp was under the direction of Frank Sturgis.

Lee said something to the effect that information on White's involvement in the assassination plot was going to be stored for safekeeping. I felt sure this material was left in the hiding place that Lee and I used in the Crescent City Garage. At any rate, I know it was in the Banister files. Lee wanted to

ROSCOE SWEENEY (r.) AND BUZ SAWYER (l.)

make sure that an unaltered version was saved, in case anything happened to him, knowing the Banister files could be
confiscated or destroyed. I never went back to the hiding place
because of the shock of the president's death. I lost no time
putting distance between myself and 544 Camp Street, and
I'm surprised that I even went back to New Orleans for a
couple of months in 1964, even though it was under a different name. I went with a friend named Nathan Bales, from
McAllen, Texas.

I am able to remember names such as Roscoe White, because I tend to associate them with something in particular.
In this case, I associated his name with Roscoe Sweeny, a very
funny and simple-looking character that I remembered from
the Buz Sawyer comic strip, which was popular when I was a
boy.

When Lee told me that Roscoe White was going to be the assassin, I laughed, and said something like, "Indeed, Lee, a man
named Roscoe is going to kill the president? What a funny name
for an assassin!" Lee knew me well enough to know I had the
comic strip character in mind, and we both laughed. Then he
tried to assure me that it was a serious matter, and that we

shouldn't be laughing. But I couldn't help it, as the thought of old patriotic Roscoe Sweeny killing the president was just too much! How soberly Lee took this, and yet I could hardly maintain my composure. Little did I know then just how serious the whole thing really was and how devastating the outcome would be.

I read a story about Roscoe White that the Associated Press published in 1990, and it helped me remember the incident. My testimony is probably the most recent evidence to link White to Kennedy's murder, and under no circumstances should it be taken lightly. Also, the word association method I utilized to remember the name so explicitly should be carefully explored.

Lee and I had a discussion about buying a car, which led to a conversation about Stephens Chevrolet, a car lot in New Orleans. He said that Jack Lawrence, a Banister confederate, was associated with the business. "Maybe I can get a good buy from him, " I said.

"No, if you ask for Jack Lawrence, they'll tell you they don't know him," Lee said. "It's an undercover thing. Don't ask for him, because they'll know the information came from me, and I'll be in deep trouble. Lawrence is supposed to be in Los Angeles." I figured he must have been on parole or something, so I decided to drop everything for the time being.

I was having a problem getting to work on time, because the conversations between Lee and me had a way of lingering on. Due to the nature of my work at the plant, it wasn't unusual to clock in as late as 8:30 or even 9:00 o'clock, but since our discussions seemed to be getting longer, Lee became concerned that I wouldn't get to work on time, and offered a solution. He asked me to come in earlier so we could have more time for discussions. He said, "You're not married, and you can leave the house any time you want, right?" I told him I could, and he said, "Well, then, can you come in half an hour earlier tomorrow?"

"Yes, I can do that, Lee," I told him. He was getting concessions out of me, but he was also playing with me. He said, "Well, if you have no wife and you could come in half an hour earlier, then you could come in two hours earlier, couldn't you?"

"I could do that too, Lee," I replied, thinking it would probably be better to get started earlier, since it was already early August, and it got hot in a hurry. I believe that Lee thought he had to maneuver me into that concession. "Good!" he responded. "There's something I want to discuss with you in the morning." Then Lee turned the conversation to the problem he had in getting away from the house, because Marina didn't like his clandestine activities and kept a close eye on him.

He said, "I don't have any problem getting out of the house early in the morning, because Marina is sleeping then. Wait till you get married, and you'll know what I mean. It's absolutely no problem for me to get out early in the morning." He told me he was about to run out of excuses with Marina when he was gone different times of the day, or in the evenings or on Saturdays. One of the excuses he used, was telling her he had gone to the movies. What made it worse was that she insisted on knowing what the movie was about, while he didn't have the slightest idea. This was amusing to him, but it had its serious side, also. It was not until 1990, when I had a discussion with Marina, that I found out Lee had been telling her he was still working at the Reily Coffee Company and would leave the house every day, just as if he were going to work.

Eventually, Marina became suspicious and decided to check up on him. She had apparently chosen to do this at the time Lee and I were in the Crescent City Garage, holding our morning discussion. When he arrived, he seemed excited and out of breath. "Marina's gonna be out front," he exclaimed.

"How do you know she's gonna be out there?" I asked.

"'Cause she's shadowing me this morning," he replied. "I've already spotted her." Lee kept glancing at his watch nervously. Suddenly, he jumped up and exclaimed, "She's out there now; I gotta go. Tell her you haven't seen me!"

"But I don't speak Russian!" I told him.

"She knows more English than you think!" he yelled, hurrying toward the back door of the garage.

I wondered how he knew Marina was already out there, but I figured he had timed her, and knew about how long it would take her to arrive. I hurried out the front door, where it seemed bright in contrast to the interior of the garage. In the process, I stumbled into a baby stroller on the sidewalk. I looked, and there was Marina, big as life, pushing June! To the best of my recollection, I apologized, and said, "Oh, excuse me," perhaps putting my hand on her shoulder. She never asked me anything, so I left well enough alone. We looked at each other with full eye contact as I slowly walked past her. Then she turned, directly facing me, as I looked back before disappearing from her sight.

In 1990, while accompanied by Larry Howard and his wife, Daryl, I visited Marina at her home in Rockwall, Texas. I asked her about our close encounter that day in front of the Crescent City Garage. "It's true I was there that morning," she told me, confirming the incident, "but I never told anyone about it, not even Lee." So it had never been documented in

REILY COFFEE COMPANY AND CRESCENT CITY GARAGE
The Reily Coffee Company was housed in the building to the right, and
the Crescent City Garage was in the lower building, just to its left, where Lee
and I met frequently, and where I bumped into Marina.

any of the publications. "I had to sell pop bottles to get enough money for bus fare to where Lee was supposed to be working," she continued, "because I'd begun to suspect that he might have lost his job." It seemed that she had walked to the coffee company and was perhaps planning to take the bus back home. She would, no doubt, be exhausted in her condition after walking more than forty blocks to check on Lee, and she apparently had only enough to ride one way. She had taken their daughter, June, and gone to check on him the morning I had seen her. She couldn't find him, but thought perhaps her inability to speak English well was the reason she was unable to make connections. Marina's admission of our encounter can be substantiated by Mr. and Mrs. Larry Howard, Oliver Stone, and Mary Ferrell.

In a telephone call that my editor and collaborator, Lessie

Young Coloma, made to Marina on December 5, 1992, Marina claimed she did not remember the encounter. This seemed odd, because in a telephone conversation between Ms. Young Coloma and Mary Ferrell, on the above date, Mrs. Ferrell said, "Marina called me in 1990 and told me of the encounter at the Crescent City Garage. She said there was no one else around besides her and Ron Lewis and the baby when it happened. She told me that she had not said anything to anyone about the incident, because she considered it insignificant."

An article in the August 25, 1991 issue of the Eugene Register-Guard, a newspaper published in Eugene, Oregon, stated the following:

'Larry Howard, co-director of the 2 1/2-year-old JFK Assassination Center in Dallas, calls Lewis' account 'absolutely credible.' Howard says Lewis told him of a brief encounter with Oswald's wife, Marina, that was undocumented in any account. Marina Oswald, he says, confirmed the incident personally to Howard. "You won't read about it in any book," he says.'

During the conversation between Mary Ferrell and my collaborator, Mrs. Ferrell was informed that Marina had denied her admission of remembering the encounter between us at the garage in August, 1963. Ferrell seemed shocked, and responded, "Oh, you're kidding! This is incredible!" She went on to say, "Marina called me in December, 1990 after Larry Howard had taken Ron Lewis to visit her. She asked me, "Mary, have you met a man named Ron Lewis?" and I told her, "Well, Yes, I met him last night." Then she asked me, "What do you think of him?" and I told her, "Marina, for some reason I believe him." then she said, "Well, I do, too."

Mrs. Ferrell told my collaborator, "It is absolutely unbelievable that she would deny it! Somebody has gotten to Marina and frightened her again. I do know that her daughters frightened her. They told her she was going to fool around and get their children killed."

This explains why Marina, after learning that I was writing this book, denied our unexpected meeting at the Crescent City Garage. She told my collaborator during the telephone interview, "When Ron Lewis visited me, I did not know he was writing a book." Mary Ferrell commented regarding Marina's statement, "That could be one of the reasons she clammed up. Marina really has been abused in some books, and probably doesn't want to be quoted anymore."

The facts show that she has been exploited and misused, and it is difficult for her to trust, to have confidence in anyone. For nearly three decades Marina and her family have lived under the shadow of the tragic events that took place in November, 1963. I certainly have empathy for Marina and her family, and I can understand how she must feel as far as defending Lee is concerned. But I cannot color the facts. She told Lessie Young Coloma during the interview that the best way to get on her good side was to present Lee as a friendly person, and she felt I was attempting to present him as a militant. Although my motive is not to present Lee as a militant, truth is truth, and the fact is that he was involved in activities of a clandestine and radical nature. Still, he was searching for something better, and perhaps he was going about it the best way he knew how. Who are we to judge?

At any rate, I was aware that Lee wanted to be an assassin, and perhaps this might seem inconsistent with my conviction that he did not shoot Kennedy. The popular consensus is that he did indeed fire the shot that snuffed out the president's life, and my statement that he wanted to be an assassin, adds fuel to that belief. However, the evidence is absolutely clear that he could not have fired a shot at the president that fateful day in Dallas.

At one of our meetings in early August, Lee had a copy of the *Louisiana Intelligence Digest*, a publication put out by Guy Banister. He was clearly fascinated with the newsletter. It appeared to be in opposition to the views he expressed, which didn't seem to bother him, as it brought out the 007 in him. Lee loved intrigue. We began discussing George Wallace, because of some feature in the *Digest*. Lee told me he hadn't read of a Wallace rally outside of Alabama, and he was keenly interested in the information I was giving him about it.

"The rally was sponsored by the Citizens Council of America, a confederate states' rights group," I informed him. I had attended one of the events in June or early July, 1963. It was given little publicity, and there were only a couple of hundred people in attendance. The only notice was a small advertisement on the second page of what I believe was the *Chattanooga Free Press*, but I never saw any follow-up in the newspaper, and I remember searching for it. It was designed to show local officials that George Wallace could be trusted to have a large rally in that town at a later date, without incident. An event of that nature, held on October 16, 1963, was widely publicized, and was basically the same as the one I had attended. I couldn't remember for sure just where this rally took place, but I believe it was in Chattanooga.

Lee told me Wallace would be a good target for an assassin, but I was neutral on the matter, so he didn't go into detail. We had not yet reached the point where he was actually divulging profound information to me. During the same conversation we talked of Medgar Evers' assassination. As time passed, we would discuss that subject more at length. Lee was indeed fascinated by assassinations, and didn't necessarily have to be involved in order to key up his interest.

At that same meeting, Lee asked if I would do some work for Mr. Banister, a CIA agent. I had already begun to see his fatal side, but I wasn't convinced that this was how he really was. He didn't stand out as being much different from any of my former acquaintances. However, as he asked me to do my first job for Banister, I was a little leery, and insisted that he describe it for me, which he readily complied with.

"Banister wants regular reports on the 'Gillis Long for Governor' rallies that are taking place in one of the local centers. There won't be any money in it," he told me, "but if you do a good job and show Banister you can make the grade, he'll see that you eventually get a good-paying job. He can manipulate that for you." Lee seemed to think money was the magic number, and that it did the trick in getting people to work for Banister. However, money wasn't what motivated me, and I made a mental note of this at the time Lee asked if I needed any money to get by on.

I accepted the job, but I had a feeling that Lee had practiced his recruiting routine at home the night before and it startled him that I accepted so quickly. I have read many accounts where he was portrayed as being destitute, but I can attest to the fact that he made me a bona fide offer of money. He indicated this by putting his hand in his pocket as if he were ready to give it to me, but I declined his offer.

"Thanks, Lee, but I'm making it okay," I told him. "My job at the plant is sufficient." My reply seemed to bother him for some reason. I'm sure he felt I would be motivated by the enticement of money, and now he would have to look for another means of motivation.

The Banister method of operation was to dispatch solely experienced persons on assignments, to send likes to likes, taking into account their leanings. For instance, he wouldn't consider sending David Ferrie to meet a Cuban operative in Canada, because it was a well-known fact that Ferrie was anti-Castro. Since Banister knew I had enough interest in politics to attend the Wallace rally on my own, he had Lee place me at the Gillis Long rally in an attempt to enlist Long in the Banister apparatus. Lee told me that at some level above Banister, data was screened to calculate feasible directives in the operation, as there was a chain-of-command that didn't end with Guy Banister or Clay Shaw. Looking back, I feel that Banister had a lengthy file under my alias, Ron Larson, although he was aware that my name was actually Ron Lewis.

I wanted to get in on the work of reporting at the Gillis Long rallies, because it brought out the military leanings that I had developed as a boy. Reporting on the governor's campaign seemed effortless and without risk. Lee gave me the address of the local center, as he had the information at his disposal. After I had made such a shambles of my life, here I was working for the government again!

THE NAZI CONNECTION

CHAPTER VI

The sun was high in the sky, but it was still cool and balmy. It was such a nice morning and Lee was so happy because of striking a deal for Banister, that he agreed to take a walk with me. I told him we would be passing a graveyard, and as we proceeded with our walk we suddenly noticed bones lying in the street and on the sidewalk. "Look, Lee," I said, "That looks like a human jaw bone!"

"It is," he said. "One thing I know about here in New Orleans is graveyards, because I've been to visit my father's grave, and I've found that rats scatter bones around." Lee went on to say, "The graves are constructed above the ground, because New Orleans is twelve to seventeen feet below sea level, so there would be a problem with water seeping in if they were below ground level." Pausing for a minute he continued, pointing to the dry, parched sidewalk. "If you would dig down right here two feet, you'd find water." I'm not sure if this was true, but that's what Lee told me. I remember the intense emotion he showed as he told me this. It was evident by his tone of voice and gestures, as if it were very important to him, and that he wanted to share it with me. But I couldn't help wondering why it meant so much to him. Why did he get so emotional about the water level in New Orleans? It's something I've always wondered about.

We continued walking, and as we passed the Lee Circle and Plaza, I mentioned to Lee that the place had his name. He said, "I've never gone there. I've always resented the name Lee, because it stands for racial segregation." I knew he was making reference to General Robert E. Lee, who commanded in the Confederate army during the Civil War. "I'll be glad when the name Lee stands for something better," he told me. "This is why I kept my name and didn't change it. If I have my way, one day it'll represent something better. Do you think I work for guys like Banister and Shaw because I Like them? No, I manipulate people like that, and ultimately I will use them." Lee's words carried a great deal of conviction.

He mentioned Marina's pregnancy, and said that when she had her baby, he would like to name it Lee.

"And if it's not a boy?" I asked him.

"Then, when you get married and have a baby boy, you'll have to name him Lee, because this is the last one I'll have," he said.

"That's a deal, Lee," I told him, shaking his hand, "If I have a boy when I get married, his name will be Lee. You can count on it!" With that, we resumed our walk.

When my first son was born in 1966, I was going to name him after Lee, but his mother wouldn't hear of it. She insisted that we name him after my alias, Kenneth Eugene, which she thought was my real name. She told me I could name the second child whatever I wanted. My next child, a son, was born in 1968, and my promise to Lee was fulfilled, since I named him Delbert Lee. His son, who is called D.J., also carries Lee's name.

During our walk that morning Lee and I talked about a variety of things, including crabbing at Lake Pontchartrain and of the Mississippi River, which was only a couple of blocks away from us; or as Lee put it, "…just out of eyeshot." We also talked about the fact that Lee's father died when Lee was only three months old. He spoke about it sadly, because he never had the opportunity to get to know him. He mentioned a picture of his father that he said he had disposed of for a certain reason. Incidentally, the collaborator of this book, while interviewing me, was able to find out the exact location of its whereabouts. There is no doubt in her mind that the photo is still there, and there will be further research concerning this matter.

We walked to within a block of the slaughter house where I worked to a grass-covered field where Lee could get a good view of the plant. Then he announced he was going to head back to Camp Street and tell Mr. Banister the good news that I was going to report on the Gillis Long rallies. I asked him to go on further to the Viking Packing Company at 346 Calliope Street, so he could see the work I did.

"No," he said, "I just wanted to see where you worked and to know that you were indeed employed here. You know, there are so many people you can't trust these days." I told him "Okay," and said I would see him later.

I didn't realize it at the time, but the information I was bringing him about Gillis, was a ground-floor plan to enlist the congressman into the Banister apparatus. They needed to be sure I wasn't connected to a rival CIA or FBI faction. Even though Lee worked for Banister, he was still his own man whenever possible, perhaps like anyone who evolves from the bottom. He had the option of placing his point of cooperation wherever he wanted. There were certain flexible pressures, and it depended on how far one could be persuaded to cooperate, or blackmailed into submission.

During our early August meetings we talked extensively of the governor's campaign. Once Lee invited me inside the structure at 544 Camp Street, since He wanted to show me the intriguing building directory. But I didn't want to go inside, because I was a fugitive and I knew it housed contract CIA offices, which made me feel ill at ease being there.

From his memory Lee listed the directory for me: "The Anti-Communist League of the Caribbeans," "Friends for a Democratic Cuba," among others. Lee was utterly fascinated by this display of international intrigue, and urged me to go into the building, but I declined. I felt the less I associated with this outfit, the better off I would be.

At first I brought him a brochure, which mentioned Gillis Long's qualifications. It stated that he had served in World War II, enlisting as a private in the infantry and rising to the rank of captain. He was awarded the Bronze Star and the Purple Heart, and had been with the internal security detachment at the trials of the Nuremberg war crimes. I was told to monitor the rallies and keep him posted. Lee told me that Gillis's detachment to internal security at those trials was of interest to Mr. Banister and his friend, Clay Shaw. He held the brochure in one hand and underlined the detachment to the Nuremberg trials with the index finger of his other hand, emphasizing its importance.

Gillis was concerned about the poor and the common workers in Louisiana. It didn't take long for him to gain my respect, and I began to attend the rallies, and became an avid supporter of his, as well. I knew this pleased Lee, because he had told me laughingly, while pointing his finger for emphasis, "Now, I know you're predictable, Ron, just like David. You have to believe in your cause!"

At that time, I asked Lee, "Why does Mr. Banister have an interest in Gillis Long?"

"Because Banister's secretary read in the newspaper that Gillis had been connected to the Nuremberg war crimes trials," he answered, "and they want to know where large caches of arms are stored that were left in Greece and other countries by the Nazis." Lee said that Banister thought because Gillis was an officer and a lawyer connected with the trials, he would have questioned Nazi officers and would know about hidden arms in these countries, making him invaluable to the cause. He also knew where arms caches under the code name "Gladio" were hidden.

As I write this book many years after the fact, it's interesting to note that Lee had access to information that wasn't exposed until after 1990. Operation Gladio was one of the projects we had discussed at length, although knowledge of its existence wasn't made public until November 1990. U.S. Intelligence recruited a large number of guerrillas, and hid weapon caches throughout Europe early in the cold war, preparing for a feared Soviet invasion. Having learned this from Lee in 1963, and from Banister indirectly, I was shocked when I read about its existence extending into the nineties. The Associated Press report, dated November 16, quoted ex-CIA director William Colby as having organized the movement in part. It brought out that the German newspaper, *Die Welt*, stated that training centers sprang up in the U.S.-occupied section after World War II. Former POWs were trained in various techniques. The report mentioned that certain weapons, etc., were stored in secret hiding places for use by the network, which had expanded throughout Europe by 1959.

These arms were of primary importance to Guy Banister and his associates, along with hidden Nazi arms. Congressman Gillis Long knew the locations of some of these weapons.

"The Nazi arms throughout Europe are cheaper than the ones here in the States since Kennedy's crackdown on arms movements," Lee told me, "and because of this, the price has gone up. Besides," he said, "these Nazi arms are new and packed in their original crates, and also have spare parts. These can get higher prices, and Ruby can get a better drug deal for their deliveries." Lee said this rather sarcastically, as he had always frowned on drugs. That was the price Banister had to pay for a man who was useful to him, who had made some very good buys, saving the apparatus substantial amounts of money. Besides, Ruby's drug-dealing could always be used against him, if the need to employ blackmail ever arose.

Lee was keenly aware of Ruby's value to Banister and his associates, and he stressed this to me several times. But it never made him very happy, because of the drug problem

Ruby had. He knew that if Ruby hadn't been greedy, he wouldn't have been in the Banister apparatus. The drug market is what kept him in tow. Lee told me he knew of a special purchase that Ruby had made. I would've paid more attention to what he said if I had known then that I would be writing this book more than twenty-five years later. All I know about the purchase was that it was made in a European country, and I can't seem to recall much more than that.

Lee had evidently overheard the Banister cronies discussing Ruby in his absence. When he mentioned Ruby's importance to Banister, he told me about the part of the discussion where Ruby made an arms purchase that saved a great deal of money. "The weapons were siphoned off from a program that supplied a secret anti-communist resistance network in Europe," Lee said. These arms were left behind by allied forces after the war, and any transactions involving them clearly became black market enterprises. It is terribly interesting to know that Lee acquired knowledge of the communist resistance network from Banister.

He told me Ruby had come from Chicago, and was with organized crime. He thought it ironic that Banister, once head of the Chicago office of the FBI, was now working with one of his former enemies. If I were quoting from a publication on the subject, perhaps what I'm saying wouldn't carry too much weight, but these words came directly from Lee Harvey Oswald. Some of these facts about Ruby have long been common knowledge, but no one knew that Lee was aware of those things. There are some who would prefer that Ruby's connections with Lee Oswald had never become known, but I must tell what I know to be true, regardless of the consequences. It seems this should be of the utmost importance to assassination researchers. There are certain ones living in this land of free speech, who might concoct a story such as this for glory, money, or some other reason. Critics may accuse me of fabricating part of this story, because I'm not coming forward with signed affidavits, but I will not compromise, regardless of the outcome.

Although Ruby was a part of Banister's dealings, he was dispensable. Even Lee spoke about him with disgust. I'm sure Ruby had a high self-esteem, being a minuteman and a right-winger, and he must have thought of himself as red, white and blue. It was his drug source that motivated him in this business of patriotism. There was no doubt that his color was "green," since he was associated with the mob, sold drugs and operated a strip joint. All this represented a great deal of money, a lot of "green" stuff. Banister found this to be quite distasteful, and as far as he was concerned, Ruby was not indispensable. Lee was a left-winger on the surface, but he once told me the political views he expressed were only a front. Lee was his own man. He could submit just what information he wanted to present to his superiors, or he could withhold it. At the time I was associated with him, he was the master of his own destiny, even though in time things were bound to change drastically.

GO GO GILLIS

CHAPTER VII

Gillis Long's cousin was Huey Long, the kingfish who had held absolute political power in Louisiana, and this led him to believe it would bring some special kind of magic in the election. Gillis desperately wanted it to be his own charisma that attracted all the attention, and not the fact that he was part of the Long legacy. He didn't appeal to the majority of White voters, as David Duke did, and the appeal to the Black vote wouldn't have been enough for him to win the campaign for governor. Gillis tended to lean toward integration instead of segregation, and in 1963 one had to be a segregationist in order to win an election in Louisiana. If only Gillis had appealed to the Whites, like David Duke did in the nineties, perhaps the outcome would have been different! It was defeating to court the Black vote in 1963.

Duke, who later became a grand wizard of the KKK, was unknown in 1963, but his current popularity shows that ties to White supremacy appeals to the grass-root Louisiana voter. Even though Duke lost his bid for the Louisiana governorship, he received fifty-five percent of the White vote. It was because Gillis appealed to the Black vote that he was defeated. Not many Blacks were registered to vote in 1963, and the Clinton project that Banister was striving to employ, was designed to discourage a Black voters registration drive. Had Gillis courted the White vote exclusively in 1963, he might have been remembered as Louisiana's governor, instead of Congressman Gillis Long. He had never been a White supremacist, but the correlation between these two time periods is interesting, seeing how this situation echoes within Louisiana today.

Not far into the election campaign, Gillis saw that the Long clan was fragmented and falling apart. Even though his cousin Russell Long, a U.S. senator, was supporting him, I discovered that his efforts were defeating to Gillis. Huey Long was the Louisiana governor who had eyes on the White House and was such a threat to President Roosevelt, with slogans such as, "Share the wealth." In reality, Gillis needed the Long Legacy, as it was the force that would determine who would be elected governor of Louisiana.

I vividly remember a billboard along one of the main New Orleans thoroughfares, that pictured Gillis at full length with briefcase in hand. It was captioned, "Go Go Gillis," and it was at one of the rallies that he revealed how he got that name. His children had dubbed him, "Go Go Gillis," because he was always telling them that he "had to go." Of course, he was referring to the times he had to go to Washington, in connection with his duties as congressman, or to Louisiana, where he was conducting a campaign for the office of governor, or wherever else it might be. He was always on the go, in between. These trips would be detrimental to the campaign, because in this case the old adage "When the cat's away, the mice do play," applied. I tried to counteract this by working extra hard, but for a campaign worker in the lower echelon, that was a major task. My job for Banister was to report on the progress of the campaign, but I was also responsible for many other duties if I intended to stay on board.

Lee had expressed a personal interest in seeing Gillis win the election, and I became a supporter that any candidate would be proud of. I was instructed to mingle at the rallies, listen for information and pick up literature. I also had to show an interest in the campaign, and in what Long stood for and planned for as governor.

I was punctual, never missed a meeting, and distributed all the literature that was assigned to me. I reported to Lee every bit of information I acquired, and later learned through David Ferrie that these reports were actually turned in. Gillis must have had an inkling as to what went on in his absence, because I remember him saying, "I know you can just take this literature home and lay it on the shelf and come back looking good, but what point would that make? If that were the case, I would rather you were working for Morrison."

The audience laughed at that remark. We were urged to take all the literature and handbills we wanted, but to make sure we put them all to good use. Gillis wasn't quite sure what to make of my presence, as rival factions were known to be present. He had referred to that in one of his speeches when he stated, "I know there is a spy here from the Morrison camp, `cause he's sitting right over there!" It suddenly dawned on me at that moment that I, too, was a spy, and was glad he pointed to the other side of the hall. I reported the spy incident to Lee, and he said, "Don't worry about him; he's one of us. His name is Hugh Ward." Incidentally, in 1964 Banister was killed at virtually the same moment as Ward and Morrison, although by different means. Banister was apparently shot in New Orleans, even though the death certificate said it was a heart attack. The other two were killed in a plane crash in Mexico. Morrison was the American ambassador to the OAS, and Ward, a Banister agent, was his pilot.

The next day Banister was thumbing through the small pile of Gillis Long leaflets on his office desk, as the squeaky air conditioner rumbled noisily in the window. The temperature was nearing one-hundred degrees and it wasn't even noon yet. Lee watched Banister closely, his boyish face anxious as he waited for his approval. "Lee, have you found someone yet to help you with the Clinton job?" Banister asked.

"You're looking at him, Guy," Lee answered, "Larson's our man. He even did some work for the NAACP in Savannah."

"Got anything else on him?" Banister asked.

"Yeah, he's wanted in Oregon for writing bad checks. His real name's Lewis, though, not Larson."

"Any relation to David Lewis?" Banister asked. "Negative," replied Lee. Banister, always pleased when he learned that Lee had the goods on someone, said, "Good boy, Lee, you're doing a bang-up job. Let's go down for coffee and ice cream."

Based on the conversations I had with Lee, that's what took

place in my absence. By the way, almost every morning that I talked to Lee, he was finishing off an ice cream cone he'd gotten from Mancuso's Restaurant. Mancuso's never opened that early in the morning, and I suspected that Lee had just gone inside and helped himself to the ice cream. One morning Lee and I were there quite early and there was no one else around, so I questioned whether he paid for his ice cream or not. He used to brag about scooping it up himself and about how much he could pile into one scoop. Occasionally, he brought one for me, and I would accept it. But most of the time if he offered me one, I acted impartial about it. I didn't like the thought of owing him anything, not even for an ice cream cone. I suppose if I hadn't shown up, he would have finished the second one off by himself since Lee was not a wasteful person, and besides, he liked ice cream.

I was uneasy about entering the building with him, because of Banister's connections. I knew that was where some of the rifles were stored, which was an illegal operation as of July, 1963, after the raid at Lake Pontchartrain. I knew the FBI was looking for me, so I preferred to meet Lee in the garage down the street, where the CIA cars were serviced. Lee knew this, and tried to use ice cream as a bribe to lure me into the edifice at 544 Camp Street. He would use the pretext of showing me the building directory or the arms shipment, any excuse he could think of to help me get over my fears of the FBI and CIA. It was Lee's assignment to recruit people like me to use in the operations, which involved alleviating my fears of these elements.

As Lee and I talked every day or so, we discussed many things besides the election. I told him of my connections with the NAACP in Savannah, including the fact that I was put in jail for racial integration actions. As the days passed, Lee's revelations gained momentum as I continued to report on the election campaign, and in the process we began building up an interesting morning dialogue. I was the only person Lee shared most of these revelations with. There was hardly anything I didn't know about Lee Oswald, including many things about his personal life.

I was attracted to girls, so naturally I enjoyed talking about the subject. But Lee appeared to be happily married, except for experiencing the normal problems that are found in most marriages, so he didn't share my interest in discussing girls. There's some speculation among researchers about what Lee's sexual preferences were, partly because of his association with David Ferrie and Clay Shaw, both known homosexuals. I feel an obligation to make it clear that in all the time I spent with Lee, I never saw any indications that he was homosexual. Besides, why would he bother getting married if that were the case?

Another time during a discussion about handing out literature on Cuba, Lee boasted that he was not afraid of the police. He was in a humorous mood, with leaflets in his hand, while keeping an eye out for possible recruits for Banister.

"There's no problem with the police before eight in the morning," Lee told me. "They're predictable, 'cause they come around at eight o'clock every morning, and if you're alert, you'll notice them." Then he took his leaflets to the outer edge of the sidewalk, held them high in his hand while flaunting himself, then yelled, defiantly, "Look, I'm not afraid of the police!"

We were laughing and carrying on. I looked at my watch in an amusing gesture and called, "Come back here, Lee, It's eight o'clock!" He knew full well that my watch didn't work, and that I was just being funny. I only wore it because it was a good-looking timepiece. Lee, feeling very defiant that morning, said in a teasing sort of way, "To hell with 'em Ron; to hell with 'em!" He didn't normally resort to such language, except when he was cutting up.

In Jackson, Mississippi, there was a racial flare-up, and Banister saw no reason for his apparatus to be involved. However, the right-wing elements he belonged to were pro-segregationist, so he had a problem. He had to be loyal either to the FBI or to the president, since he couldn't be faithful to both. To put it mildly, Banister was in a pickle!

When Medgar Evers was assassinated, Banister's superior, Clay Shaw, came down on him hard for not being in the middle of the ruckus. Clay tried to introduce military weapons into the Negro civil rights movement, as he did with the American Minutemen. With the shutting down of Operation Mongoose, munitions weren't moving, and Clay was desperate for additional clients, besides the various anti-Castro elements. They were still servicing those elements, but had planned to diversify their services because of the possible outcome of the president's orders. The real purpose of getting involved in the Black movement, though, was actually to hinder integration through COINTELPRO, which was an FBI program.

Banister was connected so profoundly to the FBI, that when he died in 1964, they confiscated the files and everything else of importance from his office. He and Shaw were deeply involved in the right-wing politics of America. The FBI was anti-integration under the direction of J. Edgar Hoover. Shaw was an important CIA contract agent, and was head of the International Trade Mart in New Orleans. However, like Banister, he was involved in right-wing factions, hand-in-hand with J. Edgar Hoover on integration issues. They were more devoted to the FBI than they were to the Kennedy administration, which were two opposing factions.

The FBI spied on those who showed an interest in existing race relations. There were no existing laws on which Banister could base his meddling in Negro voter registration drives in Clinton. Consequently, he based his actions on Hoover's cold war terminology in rooting out communists and subversives who exploited the Black movement. CORE was free of communist infiltration, and in the quest to prove that Black activists represented a communist-inspired subversive threat, the FBI, through Banister, would attempt to infiltrate a known communist into CORE in Clinton.

Lee and I were to sell arms to CORE members and be exposed as communist agitators. It was Banister's aim to exploit Lee's connection to Russia, in one way or another. But Lee had no intention of being a patsy, so he tried to involve me in the plan to dilute Banister's scheme, because I was not communist-connected. After Banister consented to Lee's idea, they were supposed to send me to Clinton, but the plan never really got off the ground, so there's no way of knowing what the outcome would have been.

THE CLINTON PROJECT

CHAPTER VIII

Lee told me of several jobs he had done for Guy Banister, and mentioned an upcoming project that was to take place in Clinton. It would pay well, and I would no longer have to work at the plant. "We are going to go to Clinton and get you an apartment," Lee said, which irritated me because I didn't like him telling me what we were going to do, since I preferred to call my own shots. I was afraid of losing my independence if I took the job, so I began looking for a way out.

There were a number of weapons that had been intended for a rebellion in France and were missed in a 1961 raid by

U.S. marshals. The uprising did not materialize, so they were earmarked for the anti-Castro community. They had to be moved from the old blimp base before Lee left for Clinton to set things up. I had my work to do at the plant and couldn't help move the arms, which didn't bother me any. Anyhow, I was expected to move to Clinton in the near future.

Jack Ruby drove the laundry truck and David and Lee followed in a car. There were two others who helped move the munitions. Banister had said, "I need two volunteers to go with these guys." Pointing to a couple of big guys, he said, "You and you," indicating which men he had in mind. They were stout men, strong and muscular, dispatched because the job was a heavy one. Banister planned his operations well. Lee told me one of the guys weighed 260 pounds. "That guy's a giant, and look at me!" he exclaimed, calling attention to his own slight build, thus justifying his reason for tiring quicker than the others.

After the arms transfer, Lee began preparing his body for what would likely be involved in hijacking a plane. He wanted to build up his endurance and develop his running ability, because he realized just how much out of shape he was when he took part in the moving job. The wooden ammunition boxes were so heavy that when I tried to lift one, I was glad I hadn't gone with them on that trip. Anyway, Banister was more interested in my mind than he was in my physical abilities. He felt he could place me in strategic positions in his operation because of the fact that I was a sharp dresser and projected an intellectual appearance.

David was Banister's top aide and Lee was his comrade, although we must remember that comrades were expendable. There were no true friendships in this business, as I would later come to realize. Lee told me that while on the moving job he was complaining of the heavy wooden boxes, and got to the point where he thought he would have to quit and appear like a weakling in front of the others. But David encouraged him, saying, "Hang in there, Lee, and give it all you've got, and the next job will be much easier!" Lee responded much like a rabbit would to a carrot on a stick. Recognizing that he was overwhelmed by the burst of strength he had gotten at that time, I asked him where it came from, and he replied, "I don't know, but I got strength from somewhere." At one time, I had toyed with Christian Science, which teaches mind-over-matter. Lee and I had discussed this several times, and I wondered if perhaps this was happening in his case. "I've been to the Christian Science Reading Room on Baronne," Lee said. "That stuff fascinates me!" Perhaps his mind told him he could lift those boxes, and he was able to do it. Who knows?

As they left the blimp base at Houma, the overloaded laundry truck containing the munitions was in the lead, with the two cars following. I asked Lee, "What if Ruby had been stopped by a policeman?"

"Then you would've read about some policeman being shot while trying to give a traffic citation," he replied. He explained that the laundry truck was a diversion, so that Ruby wouldn't be stopped. Then he added, "If a pickup had been used, it would've been sitting on the ground, with all that weight in it. At any rate, I had butterflies in my stomach all the way back to Camp Street! Marina doesn't need any more surprises like the Walker shooting!"

Lee was concerned about Marina because he had already been involved in the Walker shooting, and had promised her there wouldn't be anymore incidents of that kind. If there had been a shooting, she would've learned of this and suffered even more stress, which would have been of special concern since she was in the latter stages of pregnancy. Knowing that Marina never approved of these goings-on, and with her reaction to the Walker incident so intense, Lee never fully trusted her again. He was afraid that since she was so concerned with obeying the law, she may feel duty-bound to do something about it if she ever found out, perhaps even reporting it to the authorities. For obvious reasons Lee surely would not have wanted to see a policeman get shot the night of the arms transfer.

Lee told me that Marina was occasionally visited by the FBI, since she was Russian and married to a defector and an FBI informant. At times the FBI would come to their home and ask for Lee. On one occasion, he joined them in the car, where they talked with him at length, but when he wasn't there, they took advantage of the opportunity and talked to Marina. Lee didn't want her talking to the FBI. He felt they were playing games with him, and he wasn't willing to discuss anything with them in her presence. Although Lee was an informant, they never fully trusted him, and he knew it.

They arrived at the office and unloaded part of the shipment, putting it in Banister's office. The rest was left in the laundry truck parked at the curb. Lee was afraid of the dark and didn't want to walk home at night, so Banister gave him two dollars for bus fare, which is all the money Lee ever received from him. Banister had been to Katzenjammer's Bar down the street, while waiting for them to return with the shipment, and was a little tipsy. Lee heard Banister and Ruby talking about assassinating the president, and even though he was drunk, Lee put stock in what he said.

The next morning about seven I arrived as usual, and Lee came a couple of minutes after I did. I was sitting on the concrete-covered foundation, waiting for him to show up, when he came striding in with an anxious look on his face. "Did you see the laundry truck anywhere?" he asked.

"I've been here only a couple of minutes," I replied.

"Well, let's go look for it," he said. We looked up and down the block on Camp Street, but the vehicle was nowhere in sight. "I came here plenty early this morning and thought it would still be here," Lee commented, "but it looks like they're already gone." He seemed shaken, and visibly disappointed. Then he went on to tell me of the events that took place the night before. He felt that Ruby must have already left with the munitions, and by unloading the portion for Clinton, the truck would not be overloaded or conspicuous.

Lee had applied for a job in a local hospital in Jackson, Louisiana, but when he found out it was a mental facility, he refused to even consider working there, since he was scared senseless of insane people. Consequently, Shaw's next step was to approach Clinton instead of Jackson, as their base for this operation. Lee suspected that Banister could well exploit him in Clinton, and that COINTELPRO was designed to expose communism. He was making a bid to send me to Clinton as I was not a known communist, and he desperately wanted the project to keep a low profile, for fear of being exploited.

Clinton had a population of about 1500. I was chosen to integrate under Lee's direction into CORE, a group meeting fierce opposition from extreme racist groups, with which the Banister apparatus sympathized. My assignment was to create a militant faction, and Shaw felt because of the insurmountable opposition, the circumstances were ripe for armed conflict. The object was to agitate the situation and sell arms to the group so that the FBI could arrest CORE members and disband the attempt to register Black voters in rural Louisiana. This was in keeping with a counterintelligence program, known as COINTELPRO, designed to disrupt and destroy certain political bands. Testing the waters there, Lee, perspiring heavily, stood in the scorching Louisiana sun most of the afternoon in a voter registration line. He told me later he didn't know which was easier, loading the heavy munitions boxes or standing in the hot sun all day. Because this was the easiest of the two jobs David told him about, it was the carrot on a stick that gave Lee his strength the night of the arms transfer.

When Ferrie, Lee and Shaw got back the consensus developed that there was not enough racial tension to go ahead with Shaw's plan, so it was "no go" in rural Louisiana, and I was relieved beyond measure. I was more content to work on a volunteer basis, and continue reporting on the Gillis Long election. As I look back on the episode in Clinton and COINTELPRO, I realize that President Kennedy and the FBI were in a collision course on many issues. Banister was relieved to a degree, because the plan didn't go forward. Even though he hated CORE as much as J. Edgar Hoover did, he had predicted to Shaw that the plan wouldn't have worked, just as it wouldn't have in Jackson, Mississippi, if it had been employed there.

Banister had gone ahead with the plan for Clinton, because he had been derided hard by Shaw for missing out in Jackson, Mississippi, and there was more than just notable tension between the two of them. Now this was behind them, and they could get on with the business at hand, the proposed assassination. These events might have found their way into Banister's files under the classification number 23-7. This was Lee's personal file which also contained information on the governor's campaign and on Ron Larson.

These files were carried off in 1964 when Banister died and the FBI confiscated them. But I still made a clean break from this situation because of the embarrassment the FBI would have suffered if it became known that they were subversive against Kennedy policies. They didn't ever want the Banister files to see the light of day. Public sentiment has been expressed on opening the Warren Commission files, but the key to unraveling the mysteries surrounding the assassination lies within the Banister files. Although I hope that was not the case, they were probably destroyed by the FBI long ago.

Right after the trip to Clinton, I was told to meet David at Katzenjammer's Bar, as Lee knew I did not like to frequent the building at 544 Camp Street. Lee was continuously employing new and different techniques to alleviate my fears about going inside the place. He knew of my insecurities, because he had such idiosyncrasies himself, like his phobias of insane people and his fears of the dark ever since a buddy of his was shot and killed at Cubi Point in the Philippines.

That evening I went to Katzenjammer's Bar on Camp Street for a meeting that Lee had arranged between Guy Banister, David Ferrie and me. As soon as I stepped inside, I saw the two of them sitting at the bar, drinking. I recognized them instantly! Since it was only 5:30, we were the only people in the bar. It had been a hot day, so I ordered a Coke on ice, which to my surprise, Banister offered to pay for. He motioned with his finger to the bartender. "I've got it," he said,

KATZENJAMMER'S BAR WHERE I MET WITH GUY BANISTER AND DAVID FERRIE. (3)

"Just put it on my tab." I nodded, acknowledging the drink, but didn't approach Banister and Ferrie. Lee told me he had arranged the meeting, but I wasn't sure he had the connections to do it. However, when I was approached, I knew that all he had told me was true, including the fact that they were connected with the CIA, and that Clay Shaw and Jack Ruby were both involved in the assassination conspiracy.

Guy Banister was a commanding sort of person, so I was hesitant about approaching him directly. I was told that on the night of the arms transfer, there had been talk within the Banister organization about killing the president. But I had heard that kind of talk before in Savannah, where Kennedy was hated by segregationists, so I questioned the seriousness of it. Besides, I had been told Banister was drunk when he mentioned it to Lee, and that was another reason why I never put too much stock in it up to that point.

Thoughts such as these kept racing through my mind while I sat there, sipping my drink. Figuring I had given them enough time to approach me, I got up and went to the restroom. David must have been right behind me, since he came in immediately after I did, and it startled me. There were two things about David that bothered me. He was homosexual and he was involved in the plot to kill Kennedy, so when I turned around and saw him standing there, I felt very uneasy. I had heard horror stories of what happened to people in public restrooms, and I didn't know what to expect from David Ferrie. I realized that events of a critical nature were taking place, and I knew these people were dangerous. I had a sudden flashback of the shower room incident in prison, and even envisioned myself being found in a pool of blood on the restroom floor, killed because of what I knew! For this reason, my eyes never left David Ferrie, not even for a second!

He walked over to the lavatory, washed his hands and fussed with his wig a bit. Then he said, "Hey, you're Lee's friend aren't you?" I acknowledged that I was, and he continued, "You've been doing a damn good job at the Gillis Long rallies. We've been getting the reports, you know." So the things Lee had been telling me were true, after all! "Yes, Lee told me you were getting them," I said.

"We had a paying job for you with CORE," he said, taking a pack of Luckies from his pocket, and lighting one up, "but I guess you know it didn't materialize. The Clinton project just didn't have the potential, you know. What we want you to do is just hang in there at the Gillis Long Rallies, Ron. We've got a great deal of interest in that guy."

"I can live with that," I replied, "no problem." I told him I would continue with the rallies.

"I want you to come by my apartment and we'll discuss some options on a paying job," he told me. He gave me his address, writing it down on a paper towel. It was 3330 Louisiana, in the Parkway section of New Orleans. My biggest concern at the moment was staying able to walk out of there alive, so I agreed to see him soon. Then I left the bar abruptly without returning to my drink, wondering later if that in itself was a risky move. I couldn't afford to take any chances, so to smooth that over, I followed through on the visit with Ferrie at his apartment. In fact, many of the things I did in those days was done in order to stay alive. One such incident occurred when I went into Katzenjammer's Bar again. It was a sweltering day, and I ordered a coke on ice. "It's on the house, Ron," the bartender told me, surprisingly. I felt he obviously had some connection with Banister and that anything I told him would be passed on, so I began avoiding the place after that. I felt that I was already involved deeply enough in Banister's affairs, and didn't want to be involved any deeper in anything that might be dangerous.

At this time, events began to take place rapidly. I was one of Banister's men, and Lee wasn't actually jumping for joy about it. He liked to think of me as his man, instead of Banister's, and more than once, he said, "You're my man, Ron, and don't forget it. One day I'm going to need you!" Lee knew, however, that I would inevitably become connected to Banister, since he was only the recruiter.

It is sometimes difficult to remember the events in sequence, but what is important is that the story is being told. In fact, I am revealing much that I would actually prefer to keep hidden, because these very things could point to Lee as a prime suspect in the Kennedy murder, and I certainly do not believe that to be the case. However, I feel a profound obligation to bring this information out, and will never be able to realize a measure of peace until I do. In the next chapter I will deal with Lee's fatal obsessions.

FATAL OBSESSIONS

CHAPTER IX

After the trip to Clinton, Lee wanted me to go with him into the building on Camp Street to inspect the arms shipment. Still resisting the thought of going into an office that I believed was being used to serve the interests of law enforcement, I contemplated declining. However, Lee insisted, and having been in Banister's presence before with no adverse effects, I decided that in order to appease him I would do as he wished.

I dreaded the possibility of having to confront any of the CIA individuals when I went in with Lee. I feared that the CIA was connected to law enforcement, and since I was a fugitive,

I preferred to keep my distance. However, Lee kept telling me they were not interested in turning me in. Recruitment was very important to the apparatus, and they surely wouldn't miss an opportunity to gain a new recruit.

Everyone was out of the office when we arrived, which was obviously part of the plan in order to get me involved in their shady dealings. There were a week's accumulation of newspapers strewn on a desk, and a pair of scissors that had been used to cut out certain articles. Also, there were numerous markings on the papers that indicated which information was important. The name plate on the desk read "Delphine Roberts," and we both knew who she was. "Looks like she's going through the papers again," Lee said with a grin. Recognizing the name as that of Banister's girlfriend, I raised my eyebrows and he responded, facetiously, "Va va vous!"

Lee showed me wooden boxes of various shapes and sizes that contained foreign writing, and I commented on it. Lee, being the world traveler, laughed and replied with a grin, "Well what did you expect?" He explained that they had been originally intended for a rebellion in France, but it was over before the arms could be sent. While working on the JFK movie, I mentioned to Oliver Stone, "The writing on the boxes was in French." But he responded, "Spanish serves the theme of the movie better." So Spanish it was.

Lee, bragging about helping load such heavy boxes, told me, "Just try to lift one of those boxes!" I did as he asked, but they were too heavy. "These boxes are heavier than hell!" I said, trying to lift one end. "What's in 'em, Lee?" He became very pleased because I was showing such an interest. He told me there were hand grenades, explosives and rifles that use 30-caliber bullets, and there were several units of bullets in wooden boxes. He walked over to the squeaky air conditioner, got out his 38 revolver, waived it in the air, then put it back. "That's going to rust in there," I said, and Lee laughed. Then he walked to the files, pulled out a drawer, and with a proud look on his face, announced, "There's my file, 23-7, and here's the Gladio file 25-1. Take a good look, 'cause you'll never see these again." Before I had a chance to look them over, Lee quickly shoved them in the drawer, slamming it shut, and exclaimed, "Lets get outa' here!" He didn't have to tell me twice.

In this business if you didn't like a job, you evidently kept your mouth shut. I explained to Lee that I wouldn't have liked the job in Clinton and probably would not have done it. This bothered him, and on our way out of the office he said, "Let me tell you about a buddy of mine in the Marines." We walked to the garage and sat down on the foundation, where we made ourselves comfortable. It seemed that we should have lit up a smoke, or had a cup of coffee or something, but neither one of us were smokers, and I didn't drink coffee either, at that time.

Lee told me once that he had stolen coffee from his former employer next door, not because he was destitute, but because he enjoyed the risk involved. He had several sacks in his possession. "Want some coffee?" he asked, knowing I wasn't a coffee drinker, so I figured he said it just to be funny.

Lee's friend, Martin Schrand, was shot to death while on guard duty, and of course, I asked Lee who shot him. He answered just as I expected he would. "Well, a lot of the guys thought I shot him."

"Well, did you?" I asked.

"I can tell you right now I wasn't responsible for his death," Lee answered. "Schrand and I traveled together by car from

Jacksonville, Florida, to the radar school at Biloxi, Mississippi."

"Did you drive part of the time?" I asked. Lee fidgeted, since he had never had a license to drive, and I knew that.

"Don't you know what I'm saying, Ron? I rode with Schrand all the way to Biloxi and he was shot at Cubi Point. I thought I would get arrested for his murder. I was really scared!"

"How come you were scared if you didn't do it?" I asked. "Did you kill him?"

"I'm going to put it like this, Ron," he replied, "I'm comfortable with the decision of the Board of Inquiry. They ruled that it was an accident, and that I wasn't responsible, and I don't want to go beyond that. I like it the way it is, and that's the way I want it to stay. Wouldn't it be silly for me to admit anything more than what they ruled?"

"Whatever the case, it would be foolish to admit anything beyond the Board's favorable decision," I told him.

I suspected that Lee had killed Martin Schrand. He intended for me to get that impression, and as hard as I tried to get Lee to flat-out say he had not killed Schrand, he simply would not say it. I always had the feeling that maybe Lee took advantage of his friend's death to keep me in line, regardless of who actually killed him.

Lee continued his conversation. "This is about moving to Clinton, if they would've asked you," he told me. "I want you to know what you're involved with here. The people you report the Gillis Long information to, they play for keeps. And I like you and want you to stay alive, and for your own sake, you shouldn't forget it! They look just like you and me, ordinary guys, but if they ask you to do something for them, it's best you do it and keep on living."

I had begun to realize that blackmail and pressure from any source, was a method of their operation, and they knew I was a fugitive from justice with a strong desire to stay out of the clutches of the law. As if that weren't enough incentive to stay in line, Lee hinted strongly that he could kill a close friend easy enough, if that friend should fall out of line.

I continued to inform Lee of the Long campaign whenever we met at his office, and he was there every other day or so, and sometimes every day. Banister seemed to show an interest in three main candidates in the governor's race, although there were thirteen in all. However, those three would produce better results than any of the others.

In Louisiana, the way elections are conducted, the candidates who receive the most votes above a certain number will be in the runoff. If there is only one candidate above that number, he will be governor and there will be no runoff. In 1991, in the famous David Duke race, there were only two who came off in the election out of a large number. Whereas in 1963, there were three out of thirteen candidates in the runoff. Chep Morrison, a former New Orleans mayor and present Ambassador to the Organization of American States, seemed to be the most promising, followed by public service director John J. McKeithen and Congressman Gillis Long. The runoff would be held on December 7.

One day I mentioned to Lee the internal problems I was noticing at the rallies. When Gillis was unable to come down from Washington, his cousin Senator Russell Long, the "democratic whip," would sometimes preside, and when that was the case, he didn't help Gillis' cause at all. He would speak only of his own exploits in Washington and about his own issues, without mentioning Gillis at all. It was obvious that Russell was costing Gillis votes, and was thus damaging to him. He would tell of his famous long-winded talks before the senate, and would talk of how he could filibuster on issues that he was against. He really had a heyday before the crowd!

That was the first juicy item I had to report. The next was that a Mrs. Long was backing John J. McKeithen, who was dividing the Long camp, a blow that was devastating to Gillis. Both Lee and I assumed Mrs. Long was the widow of former Governor, Huey Long. Also there was a Speedy O. Long that would further confuse the Long camp, as he was one of the more distant candidates. At one of the rallies, Gillis said Speedy was not a relative, but I later learned that this was a campaign lie, something that I suppose is acceptable in politics. They were cousins without a doubt!

Today, as I look back on Lee's interest in the campaign, I can see that he depended on my accuracy a great deal. I had told him that Mrs. Long, widow of Huey Long, was backing McKeithen, but I was mistaken. It was instead Mrs. Earl Long, and this could have been detrimental to the wrong Mrs. Long. After all, I was not an expert on Louisiana politics, as Lee claimed to be.

We discussed the radio campaign song that Mrs. Long was portrayed on. It went, "Come on and join a rising tide,…uh-huh. Come on and join a rising tide,…uh-huh. Come on and join a rising tide…give Louisiana back it's pride,…uh-huh, uh-huh, uh-huh." Then a long spiel was given about Mrs. Long backing McKeithen for governor. From this political announcement, Lee could have ascertained which Mrs. Long was the culprit. But evidently, he paid little attention to the radio, although I do recall him saying he had listened to it.

It was evident to me that Lee had a personal interest in

Gillis winning the election, but I was uncertain just what Mr. Banister's interests were. I knew he was concerned with enlisting the congressman's help in locating arms that had been left in Europe by the Nazis, and those that were in the Gladio network. However, I told Lee the radio ad would not affect the outcome too drastically, because Gillis was bringing out the issues that would attract the voters' attention. One example was when he noted the state's lack of a retraining program for persons put out of work by automation. That pleased Lee to no end. I commented, "A song can't top that type of publicity, Lee." He replied, "I know Louisiana politics better than you do, and the only way to turn the tides in this election is to kill Mrs. Long." My God! Was this my friend, Lee, talking?

At the time I felt it was best to let him play his little games, which I didn't believe were all that serious. I figured it was just so much talk, and wanted to let it go at that. It is interesting, though, that Lee talked of killing Mrs. Long and Russell, without consulting Mr. Banister or any of the others. Lee and I believed that Mrs. Long was the wife of former Governor, Huey Long. The fact that she was not, changes nothing except the identity of who may have been the unfortunate target for Lee's obsession. Perhaps his reason for trying to involve me in the action was to find out where I stood as far as assassinations were concerned. On the other hand, perhaps it was for a different reason; who knows?

In the wake of the splintering Long political empire, former Governor Earl Long's wife, Blanche, would back McKeithen, although it wasn't clear what she was receiving in return. It was obviously something Gillis could not or would not give her, but it was a known fact that she was McKeithen's campaign manager, and he eventually won the election.

Besides the splintering of the Long faction, an issue that was detrimental to both Gillis and Chep Morrison, ambassador to the OAS, was the fact that they wouldn't join the anti-Kennedy chorus echoing within Louisiana. It might have disturbed Banister, but was acceptable to Lee. It is interesting to note that with Kennedy's death, that issue would be removed as an obstacle from in front of Long and Morrison. Kennedy was killed on November 22, and the state runoff was held on December 7. Kennedy's death would steer the Long campaign back into line with the Banister apparatus, and even Kennedy's eye had been upon this election. The March 17 edition of the Times Picayune stated, "Whoever is elected as Louisiana's governor will have a strong voice in determining whether Louisiana will be in the Kennedy column in the next presidential election." The Louisiana governor's race was, without question, observed by the White House.

Lee, continuing to advocate violence, said, "Don't feel sorry for Mrs. Long just because she's a woman. She had access to the money that disappeared from the Riggs bank box when Huey died. That money belonged to the people of Louisiana, and it's never been recovered. I tell you, Ron," he said, "I'd be justified in killing her!" Our chemistry was similar, but not to the point where I wouldn't voice an objection. For this reason I would become important to Lee by keeping him from committing violent acts.

"Killing her isn't the answer, Lee," I told him.

"Well, I wouldn't have to kill her," he said. "I could shoot at her and miss, like I did at General Walker. I chose him very carefully as a target. I knew he wouldn't be frightened out of politics the way Mrs. Long would be, but I thought he would be accused of manufacturing his attempted execution for publicity, and would therefore lose his credibility with his constituents." He said that newsmen who talked with Walker that night were convinced it was not a publicity gag. "If a splinter of the bullet hadn't lodged in the general's elbow, my plan might have worked," Lee said. Then he went on to explain how the newsmen helped to extract the splinter from Walker's elbow, so they were convinced he was telling the truth.

He was amused that the incident was investigated by the burglary division, and he assured me that burglary was not his intent. He told me he intentionally missed Walker, but I have always suspected that he meant to hit him, but was using the fact that he missed to assure me that he could miss Mrs. Long also. I wasn't buying anything that involved pointing a gun at a human being! Besides, I felt Lee might be trying to dupe me, and that he really did intend to kill her.

We got into the Walker shooting quite deeply, and it might shock researchers to know the truth about the matter, especially since there are lingering stories about a second gunman at the scene. I was told about this incident with very little held back, and nothing was mentioned about a second person being involved. However, I do remember that Lee told the story with a lot of mirth, because he was mistaken for a security guard by a couple of young trespassers in a late model Ford. "When I fired the shot, two boys jumped up out of nowhere and ran like they'd seen a ghost," Lee said, "and I didn't even know they were there until I fired at Walker. They jumped in their car and peeled out like a bat outa' hell!"

"Did those guys ever go to the police about it?" I asked.

"No," he replied, "I guess they were too scared. They never did come forward as witnesses, at least they haven't done it yet." Perhaps they never read the newspaper, and weren't aware of what had actually happened, or maybe they just didn't want to get involved. I realize this shoots down some theories, but I have to tell it the way it was, exactly as Lee told it to me. I know there has been some speculation about the two boys being involved in the shooting incident, but that is not the case.

As our discussion turned to Russell, Lee said he was one of the first politicians to oppose Castro, and that he had caused Cubans to suffer when he advocated revision of the sugar quota to counter Castro's drive toward communism. As one of Banister's agents attending the Gillis Long rallies, I was interested in where he got his information on Russell Long, since I was quite involved in the campaign. Surprisingly, he told me his source. Lee was quite a know-it-all, and I expected him to say something like, "It just came to me naturally." But, instead, he told me, "I read it in a book called *The Huey Long Murder Case,* and if you want to be up-to-date on it, you should check it out and read it."

"I don't have a library card and I don't want to get one," I told him, "since I don't have any I.D. under the name I'm using." "No problem, Ron," he responded, handing me a library card. I looked at it, and it had David Ferrie's name on it. Handing it back, I said, "I've been spending Saturdays at the library, and I'll read it this weekend."

Lee had a certain smugness about him because of having David's card. This stands out in my memory because it was only a card. If I had something similar that belonged to a friend, I wouldn't think it was such a big deal. But Lee put special emphasis on having it, maybe because David was deeply entangled in CIA affairs, and that was something he idolized.

As our conversation changed from David Ferrie to Russell

Long, Lee said, "Russell should be shot, and given the opportunity, I'll do the job myself. I still have the rifle at my house that I used on General Walker. You wanna go see it, Ron?" he asked. "I'll pass, Lee," I told him, "you live a long way from here."

Lee shared all this information with me during one morning's conversation, and He hadn't consulted Banister or anyone else about any of his notions. Lee's ideas at this point were products of his own thinking, and he certainly had the capability of acting upon them.

KILL FOR VENGEANCE AND DIG
TWO GRAVES

CHAPTER X

There's no doubt that Lee wanted to be an assassin. It disturbs me to admit that, because there are many who believe he assassinated President Kennedy, and I do not want to add fuel to that theory. In August Lee was desperately seeking a target, and we had already discussed a few men who had set themselves up as targets, including General Walker, Medgar Evers and George Wallace. But I didn't realize the depth of the mental conflict within him until later.

A matter of disagreement existed between Lee and me, but we kept it on a jovial scale, joking about it. Lee enjoyed reading James Bond novels, and I refused to read them because they were fiction. He continually tried to convince me the novels were useful to him in his dealings, and it remained a point of controversy between us. I think I first learned of this during the same conversation in which he told me of his desire to eliminate the Longs. During our discussion of the novel, *With Love, From Russia,* Lee told me, "If you read any of the novels, you shouldn't read that one." He might have said it because he thought that particular novel would turn me off on the rest of them. Whatever his reason, he mentioned that there were many helpful things he got out of reading the Bond novels. One such instance was when he discovered the quote, "When you kill for vengeance, you dig two graves." While doing research I came across the book, *For Your Eyes Only,* and found the passage, "...you know what they say in China; before you set out on revenge, dig two graves. Have you done that, or did you expect to get away with it?" (4) This book was published in 1962.

Afterwards, our conversation turned to the 1962 gubernatorial race between Walker and Connally. Lee explained that because of Connally's apathy on his discharge issue, he considered shooting him, but at the time he was unaware of the risk. "There are many reasons why Connally should be shot besides my own personal reasons," Lee said, "but if he were ever shot, I wouldn't want to be within the range of suspicion in the incident." Then expounding on his theory, he said, "I should've taken a shot at Connally instead of Walker, but I'm glad I didn't, because later on in the novel, I read, "When you kill for vengeance, you dig two graves." I asked him how that was possible, and he answered, "When you kill for vengeance, there are strings that can tie you to the crime. I wrote Connally a letter concerning my discharge, and received a letter from him, begging off his responsibility. You know…I left a paper trail. If Connally is ever shot, I don't want to be in the area, as the letter would incriminate me." When I shot at Walker, there were no previous dealings that tied me to the occurrence, and this is why I'm walking around free today, even though the incident was quite serious." Lee was serious as he said, "Here I am with reason to shoot Connally, and yet I'm his guardian. If I thought you were going to shoot him, I would have to stop you!" That's how intense Lee's feelings were about it. It is interesting to note that even now, Connally does not believe he was a target on that fateful day.

I don't think those revelations alarmed me much, since no one had ever been assassinated by Lee. Even his talk about killing the Longs didn't really alarm me, but his admission to the attempted shooting of General Walker was another matter, and it did have quite an impact on me. The issue that kept cropping up in my mind was the distinct possibility that Lee might be dangerous, and I realized that I knew far too much about him and his past, and it worried me.

Concerning the Longs, I didn't approve of the way Lee wanted to handle the election, and I tried to discourage him from any possible foolish acts in a way that wouldn't hurt his feelings. I felt that whoever was to be the next governor of Louisiana, should be determined by popular vote and not by Lee Oswald, alone. This concern began to weigh heavily on my mind, and I thought about it often during the dark, quiet hours of the hot summer nights.

I remember exactly the reasoning I used in being apathetic about taking the Long revelation seriously. I was searching deeply within myself and within the existing situation for a reason not to get alarmed, and I found one I can remember as clearly as if it were yesterday. Although they worked together, I realized that Lee and Banister were political opposites and that Banister would not display such animosity toward the Longs. I believed he would unwittingly serve as Lee's monitor. I felt if I just left the situation alone, it might correct itself in time, but I was wrong. It was clear as I continued to monitor it that I had miscalculated. Certainly Lee had been searching for a target, and it seemed he had found one. It would be all I could do to prevent something tragic from happening. There were other circumstances that also played a part in preventing such an act. One was the fact that Russell wasn't at the rally the night Lee was out with his rifle. However, Senator Long's life hung in jeopardy for about a month that summer. While I continued to report events connected with the Gillis Long campaign, I tried to keep from revealing things that would fuel Lee's fatal ambitions.

Shortly after the morning Lee had shown such animosity toward the Longs, I attended a Gillis Long rally. I was just stepping out my door on Iberville Street, when I saw Lee walking rapidly in the direction of town, where the rally was scheduled to take place. He was carrying an awkward, green package under his arm, and I recognized it by its oblong shape. It was his rifle. I had no idea what he was doing in the vicinity of my house, but he was coming from a direction that indicated he had either been to the mid-city area, or else was possibly just circling my block. It aroused my curiosity, because he didn't live in that area or in that general vicinity.

When I arrived at the rally, I was relieved to find out that Russell wasn't able to attend that night, and that Mayor Shiro was officiating. I can remember hoping, and I mean a real gut hope, that Lee didn't hold a grudge against the Mayor. As I sat there perspiring in the August evening's sweltering heat, I noticed that the door in the hall to our rear had been left open. I looked back occasionally to see if I could see Lee anywhere, but I couldn't continue looking back without arousing the suspicions of everyone around me.

My mind has always played tricks on me as to whether or not I actually saw him standing in the doorway when I looked back. However, when I saw him that evening across the street from my house, I yelled at him twice. "Hey, Lee! Lee!" I hollered, but he didn't answer, which led me to believe that he had his rifle with him.

Anyhow, I was disturbed enough about the incident that the very next day I went to a public telephone booth so I could check the directory to see if Mrs. Long lived in that direction. I couldn't find her name listed but the curiosity remained with me. I had truly expected an attempt to be made on the senator's life the night before, and I was happy that Long didn't show up.

Shortly after the incident I had a telephone installed in my apartment. I have since tried to find out if the number was ever listed in the directory, but evidently I didn't have it long enough for it to be listed. At any rate, in November I left New Orleans owing a phone bill.

I began to take personal precautions and stay indoors at night. With thoughts of what happened to General Walker always in the back of my mind, I now turned my lights off after dark. There was a cockroach problem in the area and I had to take the garbage out every evening, but from that time on, I always waited until after daylight to take it out. I was afraid Lee might have second thoughts about confiding in me that he had shot at General Walker, and decide to do something foolish, which could cost me my life.

The next morning when I saw Lee, I mentioned that I'd seen him passing my house the night before. "I called you, but you didn't answer," I told him, "What was happening?"

"I was definitely in that area on some business, but I didn't hear you," he replied casually. I knew he had heard me, but I never questioned what he told me, because in the Banister apparatus, asking questions about things that didn't concern you was a "no-no," and I certainly didn't want to rock the boat. I was worried about what Lee might decide to do to me, considering all I knew about him. However, because I was a fugitive and a captive audience, he may have thought his secrets were safe with me. My fears subsided somewhat, as I began to realize that Lee was unlikely to harm me, since he had no doubt learned by this time that he could have the utmost confidence in me.

From consulting the available record, including various books on the subject, and from my own personal knowledge, I have come to realize that Lee spent his evenings at home with Marina and the baby, except on rare occasions. It appears he spent the weekends in much the same manner. If he did a certain thing one day, he would tell me about it the next, unless it was on a day we didn't meet, and then he would bring me up-to-date at our next meeting. As it was, he provided me with much more information than I gave him. In pinpointing the evening I saw him out with the rifle, I've learned to use some of the other publications, such as *Marina and Lee*, by McMillan. It states:

> *One evening during the last week of August, she (Marina) and June went for a stroll.*

Usually, Lee went with them on these evening strolls but this was a special night for him, since he was going to shoot Senator Russell Long. He left the house with the makeshift package containing the rifle, and he knew he had until twilight of the long, hot summer evening before he had to return, so Marina wouldn't know he'd been out. He would have to take a bus home, because it was quite a distance. I know, because I have checked it out.

The rally started about 7:30 P.M., and I was just stepping out my door around 7:10, so Lee must have left his house the moment Marina left for the stroll, since he passed by my place at that time. For some reason he must have circled my block, which was a bit off the path that he normally would have taken to the rally. Lee walked very fast and was a long-legged guy, so I wasn't able to catch up with him. He always had to slow down for me when we walked together. I sensed that he didn't want to encounter me, so he disappeared, and I suspect he turned off somewhere to avoid me. I strongly feel that he went to the rally, and found Russell wasn't there, so he went on home, arriving just ahead of Marina. He was very likely on a high that he had always gotten from such an occasion. Now to continue the narration from *Marina and Lee*, by McMillan:

> *Arriving home about twilight, they found Lee on the porch perched on one knee, pointing his rifle toward the street. It was the first time she had seen him with his rifle in months...and she was horrified. "What are you doing?"*
> *"Don't talk to me. Get on about your own affairs." (5)*

After this, Lee could be found out on the porch, practicing with his rifle. He told Marina it was to help Uncle Fidel, a handy excuse he used to pacify her. Marina said he did this until the middle of September.

However, it was on September 7 that Castro made the alignment statement in Havana that in part, caused Lee to become involved in the conspiracy at 544 Camp Street. This is when his other entanglements began to come to a halt, and he became active in the participation.

Lee used fluent body language and hand gestures, which made him interesting to talk to. Since Stone and I were also anti-establishment, he held our interest. He kidded around a lot like he did when we were in Dallas. His mirth seemed to be somehow tied in with the serious part of his conversation. For instance, once he told me he had aspirations of one day becoming prime minister of the United States. "One day I'll be Prime Minister Lee Oswald!" he said. When he said this, he was kidding around, yet serious. He knew that the U.S. had no prime minister, and seeing that he had mentioned this to Marina also, I think he used the line as an eyebrow-raiser.

The firing capabilities of Lee Harvey Oswald were tested prior to August 22, 1963. However, it was not a Mannlicher-Carcano rifle that was used, as some believe. He used a general-issued rifle at the training camp, and the results were placed in Banister's office files under the classification 23-7, which was confiscated by the FBI in 1964. Lee went with David Ferrie to the Pontchartrain secret training base, which had been shut down by federal marshals, but was still open. He practiced shooting rifles and did some training with the anti-Castros. He told me that was the only time he had ever gone there. Their purpose in going was to practice and to get Lee's score on record. Lee placed his own score in Banister's file cabinet under the classification 23-7, even though Banister told him it wasn't necessary. However, Lee wanted it on file for future reference.

I asked what his score was, and he replied, in a playful way, "You knew I was a Marine didn't you?" I planned to just leave it at that, but later he said, "I want to tell you because you may hear about my score. Anyway, I could have done better, but I purposely missed a couple of shots. The rest of them were bull's eyes! When I have to use my rifle it will be on my terms, not theirs."

Before September 7 Lee seemed to be the master of his own destiny. The best way to get out of the assassination plot was to be a lousy shot. His plan would ultimately backfire, though, because he was destined to serve the Banister apparatus in some capacity, even if it were only as a patsy. Lee didn't trust Banister, and he knew he was involved with high-risk adventure, but he assured me he had everything under control. He felt confident he could handle them in the final showdown. Only the expression on his face betrayed that confidence when he was gunned down by Jack Ruby. In that final moment, as he lapsed into unconsciousness, he realized he had played a game of the highest risk, and had come off the loser.

I had firsthand knowledge of leaflets left in Mr. Banister's office, which were found in 1964. At one point, when Lee and I were talking about distributing leaflets at the Camp Street address, he told me, "When I first handed them out in July, I began at the Lafayette entrance. Mr. Banister caught me, and snatched them away from me. He was absolutely furious!" Lee said Banister yelled at him, using a few choice words. "For shit's sake, Lee! Can't you do anything right?" Banister asked, "I said the other entrance!" So Lee continued to distribute them at the Camp Street entrance, which didn't bother Banister, since it had been previously arranged. Lee and I began distributing at that location, where I handed out a leaflet, and for some reason Mr. Banister happened to be on hand. He looked me in the eye with a frigid stare, one of the few times I had seen him face-to-face.

I wondered what Banister was really like. I didn't know whether to imagine him as a kindly uncle, as Lee first portrayed him, or as a certain Captain Herder from my prison days. As I mentioned earlier, Lee told me that on the night of the arms transfer, when he gave him the two dollars for bus fare, Banister was drinking heavily at Katzenjammer's Bar on Camp Street, while waiting for the arms to arrive, and was very tipsy. "No one gets in his way when he's like that," Lee said.

"Have you gotten your leaflets back from Mr. Banister yet?" I asked. He answered, "I've been in his office several times, but he hasn't offered to give them back, so I haven't asked for them." I surmised that this had something to do with just letting the issue lie.

I read in later publications that, upon Mr. Banister's death in 1964, the FBI took everything of importance from his office, but overlooked the stack of Fair Play for Cuba leaflets. When Mrs. Banister finished cleaning out his office, she wondered what the significance of those leaflets was. They were in Banister's possession because Lee had distributed them on Lafayette Street, and that irritated him. He took them away from Lee in anger, and never gave them back.

In August, around the 20th or 21st, Lee told me he was going to be on a radio debate over WDSU. He mentioned that it might get sticky, because his opponents were intent on smearing him, perhaps telling things about him that I might not even know about. He was unsure what they might bring out against him, and he was worried. He wasn't so concerned about what the people of New Orleans would think, as he couldn't have cared less about what people thought of him. But he had one friend, only one friend in the whole world that seemed to truly care about what happened to Lee Harvey Oswald, and he didn't want to jeopardize that friendship! Can you imagine what it would be like not to have even one friend in your entire life? This is what Lee's life had been like. He couldn't even trust George de Morenschildt. He desperately wanted to, but couldn't even tell him he had shot at General Walker, unless he used an approach on the order of a riddle.

By this time I knew I was Lee's only friend, and he was afraid that the radio broadcast would turn me against him. He wanted me to listen to it, but knew he wasn't going to gain any popularity. He was really worried that I would desert him, as he liked to think of me as an ally rather than someone who was just one of Banister's people.

"Ron, I want to talk to you in the morning after the debate," Lee informed me, "and if you don't meet me at the usual place, I'll have to come by your apartment to find out why you didn't come." He told me in no uncertain terms that he would be knocking on my door if I ever attempted to skip out on him. He continued, "If you don't like what they say about me, please give me a chance to explain my side of the story, because I might not get that chance on the radio."

"Don't worry, Lee," I assured him, "I'll be here tomorrow morning… same time, same place!"

After the Walker incident, I was nervous about the thought of Lee coming to my house, as I had no way of knowing what it might entail. The fact that he had a rifle and a handgun made me a little edgy. So did my knowledge of his intentions toward the Longs, and also the information he had passed on to me about his Marine Corps friend who was killed at Cubi Point. Knowing about Lee's fatal obsessions made me a little apprehensive about him coming to my house to explain his side of the story. I agreed to meet him as he wanted, although he had already said enough that caused me to begin distrusting him. Furthermore, I knew what he was capable of.

I turned on the radio and soon the broadcast began. My memories of that evening are mostly about myself. I seemed to be halfway around the world from where my roots were, deeply involved with a revolutionist that happened to be the only friend I had. I saw nothing improper or dangerous about my friendship with Lee or my work for Banister. But there was something about this broadcast that opened my eyes to just who Lee Oswald really was, and just what he was actually taking on. One issue was the U.S. policy toward Cuba, by far his biggest project since his Russian adventure. Needless to say, this was a dangerous position in 1963.

Lee's known opponent was an anti-Castro refugee, a militant who had frequented 544 Camp Street. As it turned out, however, those who made up the broadcast panel brought out the fact that Lee was a communist who had turned his back on America and defected to Russia, something he had tried to keep under wraps. Lee hit the nail right on the head when he said I might not want to continue my relationship with him after listening to the broadcast, but I had no choice. I was in too deep to just walk out. However, I began to make contingency plans since I was involved in something I hadn't intended to get into, and I hoped I would eventually find a way out.

I can remember Lee telling me, "I would rather have lived a lifestyle like my brothers, where I wasn't committed to anything but a job and family, leaving politics out of my life." If this had been the case, Lee would never have been involved in such radical maneuvers. But it was too late! He could never change the past. What had happened was already water under the bridge, and when he fired the shot at General Walker, he knew there was no turning back.

Perhaps he could have lived down the defection to Russia, because something good had come out of it. He had met Marina and married her, and now they had the baby and another one on the way. But he had gone too far and talked too much, and now Mr. Banister knew of his attempt to kill Walker. Lee cursed himself many times over for not being able to keep his mouth shut. He said, "You just wait, Ron. The time will come when they'll use that against me."

On the evening of August 21, 1963, Lee Oswald walked into the reception room of radio station WDSU in New Orleans to do an interview with Bill Stuckey and the program's moderator, Bill Slatter. It turned out to be his famous radio debate.

Lee wore a heavy gray flannel suit, much too hot for the sweltering August weather. He was perspiring and slightly nervous as he met a battery of people, preparing for the interview. Participants were Bill Stuckey, Bill Slatter, Carlos Bringuier, an anti-Castro faction leader, and Edward Scannell Butler, executive vice-president of The Information Council of the Americas, or "INCA." This was an anti-communist organization that made what was commonly referred to as truth tapes, to be rebroadcast in Latin American countries.

While waiting for the broadcast to begin, Stuckey, Slatter,

and Butler contemplated their attack on Lee, and Lee and Bringuier engaged in conversation. The two of them had formerly had a disagreement, and Lee ended up in jail for disturbing the peace. Carlos said, "Listen, Mr. Oswald, I would like to explain to you that other than the troubles between you and me and our ideological differences, I don't have anything against you as a person. Communism is trying to destroy Western civilization, and principally the United States. Maybe you are mistaken in good faith" (6).

Lee responded, "I am sure that I'm right and you're wrong." He paused briefly, then continued. "I see, Carlos, you have the Marine Handbook I gave you. You don't have to carry it around anymore, and I sure hope you don't organize any expeditions against Cuba on the merits of that book, because it's out of date" (7).

With limited time for small talk, the debate got under way. As I sat in my apartment at 1923 Iberville, I listened to every word carefully. On the program, Lee displayed brilliance seldom equaled by anyone his age. It's possible that because of certain copyright laws, the public has been deprived of demonstrations of his outstanding abilities. These abilities were brought out strongly on the program. The radio station was WDSU and the program was called "CONVERSATION CARTE BLANCHE." Bill Slatter began the program by greeting the listeners and identifying who Lee and the other guests were. Stuckey elaborated on the background of the Fair Play for Cuba Committee and Lee's activities in New Orleans. It seemed the cardinal point was to prove that Lee and the FPCC were communist-controlled. Referring to newspaper clippings, he asked Lee if he had lived in Russia for three years.

"Mr. Oswald, are they correct?" he asked.

"That is correct." Lee answered.

Bringuire asked him which one he belonged to, the Fair Play for Cuba Committee or the Fair Play for Russia Committee.

"That is provocative and doesn't require an answer," Lee shot back. Bringuire replied at length in his broken English, pointing out that before the revolution, Cubans were better off than the Russians. And now that Cuba was selling its sugar to Russia, they were getting paid in junk instead of in the dollars they had been paid by the United States. There were a couple of points that would stick with me throughout the years about this broadcast. One was the number of members that Lee had in his organization. I was afraid he would mention me, but I breathed a sigh of relief when he didn't.

"How many members do you have in your chapter in New Orleans?" he was asked.

"I can't reveal this," Lee answered.

"Is it a secret society?" Butler inquired.

Lee's answer was another point I remembered because of his brilliant response. "It's standard operating procedure for a critical, political minority to safeguard the names and numbers of its members," he replied.

Butler, who seemed to be a critical snip of a man, replied that the Republicans were a minority, and he didn't see them hiding their membership. But Lee responded that the Republicans didn't represent a radical point of view. "They don't have a violent and emotional opposition, as does the FPCC," he said.

Butler didn't let that stop him. "Well then, would you say it's a communist-front organization?" he asked.

Lee's reply was keen and consistent. "The senate sub-committee that investigated us from several points of view, has found no subversion, as you suggest."

They attempted to badger Lee and repudiate his statements, but he held fast to his convictions. They accused him of trying to renounce his U.S. citizenship. He tried to sidestep the issue, but they wouldn't leave him alone. The Washington Evening Star was even quoted, to show that he had applied for Soviet citizenship. "Well, your answer is obvious," he told them, "A person who renounces his citizenship is legally disqualified to return to this country, and I am back here in the United States!" I have always been amazed at Lee's intelligence, especially since he was only twenty-three!

Mr. Stuckey was interviewed by David Barron of the *Raleigh North Carolina News and Observer* on November 22, 1989. Stuckey was critical of the police for arresting Oswald and placing him in jail for being the victim in an altercation with Cuban refugees. He said simply, "That's New Orleans." Stuckey admitted, "We savaged him on the show, as two anti-communists tried to debauch his views." After the program, he took Lee out for a beer. Mr. Stuckey admitted that he was beginning to hate New Orleans for its conservative ways.

When they said Lee would be in the hot seat that night, they were right on the money! In my opinion presidential debates, such as the one I witnessed between Nixon and Kennedy, weren't as interesting as Carte Blanche was that evening. Visualizing Cuban exiles glued to the radio in David Ferrie's apartment, I turned my radio off and wrote down the high points of the debate.

The next morning I went to work early because I knew Lee would be eager to know what I thought of his first radio debate. When I got to his office he was there, sleepy-eyed and yawning. He said he had been out to a bar with the producer after the show, and had stayed out quite late. He was still concerned about my reaction to the debate, and perhaps even worried that I might not show up, so he had gotten out of bed early and met me at his office. "You did real well for the way those guys attacked you," I commented.

"At any rate, I did most of the talking," he replied, "and isn't that what counts? That kind of exposure costs Mrs. Long good money." He continued, using expressive body language, "I get it done for nothing," It had been a few days since he had mentioned Mrs. Long, perhaps because the debate had occupied so much of his mental processes.

Just a couple of days after the debate, he came up with one of his bombshells that he sometimes dropped out of the blue, such as his admission of the Walker shooting. "I'm going to hijack a plane to Cuba and I'll need your help," he told me. He had been exercising to build up his stamina for the job, and demonstrated by running from one side of the garage to the other and back again, just to show me how fast he could run. It was quite humorous to watch him zigzagging back and forth like that. He was wearing a white T-shirt, gray pants and street shoes, and he tried to be funny and at the same time serious. Needless to say, he looked comical. "Are you really looking to me for help, Lee?" I asked.

"You know I don't have anyone else," he answered, "Marina can't shoot a gun, and besides, she's already as big as a blimp. Don't you see? I've got no one else to help me."

As I began to realize Lee was serious, my mind wandered to various headlines of previous hijacking incidents. I always wondered what type of people engaged in such risky escapades, and what prompted them to commit these desperate acts. Now I was able to understand more of what made them tick. But what were Lee's underlying reasons for such desperation? I just couldn't put my finger on it. I only knew I didn't want any part of it, and had to try some kind of strategy to get out of it, hoping not to offend him. I felt a great deal of empathy for him because of his principles and the insurmountable odds against them ever being applied.

Lee's stand against segregation looked bleak even in 1963, especially in New Orleans where the courts provided a colored section. Yes, I pitied him, but I saw no reason for hijacking a plane. That was out. "Well, Lee, you know how important the Gillis Long campaign has become to me," I told him. "I admit that you got me interested in it, but Gillis now has so many obstacles confronting him...like the problem with Russell and Mrs. Long, and the split in the Long faction. Don't you think it's logical for me to stay here and finish the campaign?"

"Ron, they're talking about killing the president in there!" Lee exclaimed.

"Who is?" I asked.

"They are, the whole bunch...and Ruby's there, too. There's even a guy named Roscoe White that's to infiltrate the police department, like we were to do with CORE, and they're planning on my help."

Reily Coffee Company was just next door and the aroma of coffee was always in the air. "Come on, Lee, wake up and smell the coffee," I said.

"I'm not just whistlin' Dixie, Ron," Lee replied seriously, "this whole thing has the backing of the government. They expect me to help them, and we don't dare tell anyone about it but Kennedy himself."

"How do you know they want your help?" I asked.

THE CELL LEE WAS HELD IN AFTER HIS ARREST, FOLLOWING THE ASSASSINATION.

"The other day Banister asked me where my rifle was," he answered. "I lied to him and said it was in Dallas buried in plastic covering beneath some bushes at my old Neely Street address. Don't tell anyone it's really at my apartment. You're the only one who knows that, so I'll know where it came from if I hear it mentioned."

"Is Mrs. Roberts in on it, too?" I asked.

"Oh no, don't ever say anything about that to her," Lee said, indicating that Mrs. Roberts, Banister's secretary and girlfriend, was not in on the conspiracy.

On the night of November 22, 1963 at Lee's late-night press conference, he was accompanied by a magazine photographer, Jerry Herald, in the elevator on the way back to his cell.

"Listen Jerry, I didn't shoot the president," Lee told Herald, "I'm taking the blame for others, and the truth about the assassination conspiracy will be brought out at the trial (8)." I have always wondered why no one ever followed through on this particular testimony.

Ruby helped move the munitions from the old blimp base, and was responsible for seeing that they got to their destination. Banister was undecided about where to send them.

"Let's send 'em to Cuba, Guy," Ruby said.

"Like hell, Jack. I need this stuff at the lake," Ferrie objected. Ruby loved to deliver arms to Cuba, because he received drugs in return. Lee didn't tell me exactly how the deliveries were made, but I knew they came in to Miami and then were transported by car to Dallas. He was amused that Ruby lost his bid for the arms. "No drugs that time," Lee told me.

"I thought Banister was against drugs," I told him.

"He is," Lee replied. "This is just something he knows about and files away for additional pressure when more cooperation is needed." I was learning the hard way; this was Banister's method of operation. He continued to be alarmed about the assassination plan.

"I've heard the Kennedy death threat before, and nothing's happened yet," I assured Lee. "That sort of thing was an everyday occurrence in Savannah, but it won't happen here."

"Well, I'm not going to sleep good tonight," he remarked. "I've got nothing against Kennedy; he's being as fair to Castro as anyone I know. Really, he's being more fair than Banister and the rest, because they'll sell guns to the refugees just as fast as they sold them to Castro in the old days."

As time passed, I tried to tell Lee it was only talk, that they were just disgusted because Kennedy was stopping Alpha 66, and had attempted to close the base at the lake. "Don't get worked up over nothing," I told him, but I could not convince him that all the talk was without basis. He said they hadn't anticipated acceptance of integration, and of practically surrendering to Castro, as well as a pull-out of Vietnam. They knew the missiles moved out of Cuba were those the Russians had intended for the United States to find, mere decoys. Kennedy knew it would be politically unwise to tell the American people there were still Russian missiles in Cuba. It was better to keep the people in the dark concerning this situation, until after the election.

"Yes, Banister and his cronies are really planning to assassinate the president," Lee said, with concern, "these things bother them a lot." In fact, what infuriated Banister and his cronies the most was the fact that Kennedy had allowed the missiles to remain in Cuba. Kennedy knew from the intelligence report that David Ferrie and Robert Morrow had supplied them from their pre-dawn mission to Cuba on April 17, 1961, a flight I was told about in August 1963. It confirmed there were Russian missiles in Cuba, and subsequently the U-2 flights commenced. When a few missile containers were spotted aboard Russian vessels leaving Cuba, Banister was infuriated, because he knew the missiles being transported were decoys. He suspected there were still missiles in Cuba, and discovered they were there openly, indicating they had Kennedy's blessing.

Banister also believed the Bay of Pigs invasion was used as a diversion tactic to insure the success of the intelligence flight into Cuba to discover the missiles. Kennedy couldn't curtail the plans for a Cuban invasion, which he inherited from the former administration, and it was Banister's belief that he ordered the invasion as a cover for Ferrie's flight. He then refused air cover in a calculated failure as payment to the Soviet Union for political maneuvering on a global scale. This was the consensus at 544 Camp Street.

Banister and Shaw were critical of the size of the diversion and the loss of life, and of the fact that air cover was not provided to insure its success. They felt that if it were a calculated failure, the expense was too great; that a hit-and-run by Alpha 66 would have been a sufficient diversion with minimal loss. However, regardless of the expense, it was the Banister belief that the Kennedy administration decided to suppress the information from the American people for personal and political reasons until after his re-election bid.

We can gain a little insight into Banister's world by considering some things in retrospect, by looking into the undelivered presidential speech that was to be given by Kennedy in Dallas on November 22, 1963.

> *"America today is stronger than ever before. Our adversaries have not abandoned their ambitions, our dangers have not diminished—our vigilance cannot be relaxed. But now we have the military, the scientific and the economic strength to do whatever must be done for the preservation and promotion of freedom." (9)*

By leaving the missiles in Cuba, regardless of what motivated him, Kennedy's vigilance was relaxed, and the American people were at risk. According to Lee, this more than any other reason was what motivated the Banister apparatus to arrange the assassination. To a certain segment of the American government, Kennedy now represented a national security risk.

"I heard all this in Savannah, and nothing happened, and nothing will come of it here either," I told Lee over and over, trying to reassure him. "Just ride it out and everything will be all right." I was really convinced of that, and I told him, "They'll cool off in time."

After Lee's attempt to convince me that a plot existed to kill the president, I walked on to work, with things we had talked about weighing heavily on my mind. It was a relief to occupy myself putting meat in the smokehouse and doing all the other things I was required to do in the course of a day's employment. Things such as the election, the hijackers, gun-runners and drug traffickers would all soon fade into oblivion.

While walking home that evening, I took a good look at 544 Camp street. The building was long and rather narrow, and was made of deteriorating brick, which reminded me of B block in prison. It was erected in the 1800s, with Mancuso's Restaurant nestled in its bosom, and in close proximity to Lafayette Square situated beyond Camp Street. There was a wino fast asleep in the warm afternoon sun, and several pigeons were pecking away at something near him. It seemed like a beautiful day to just sit in the park and meditate on my circumstance, with streetcars going by in the distance, and thoughts of my friend, Lee, prevalent in my mind. Lost in my reverie, that's how I spent the afternoon.

As my contingency plan began to unfold in my mind while sitting there in Lafayette Square, I entertained the possibility that Lee's accusations might be true, and if they were, what should I do? I was in a bad position, and needed an alternate course to follow if the need should arise.

I was reading a magazine a few days earlier that had a pen-pal column in it. It contained the name of a Mexican girl from Harlengen, Texas, and I decided to write to her, and if necessary, use this as a contingent plan. After sending off the letter I waited for a response, not mentioning anything to Lee nor telling him that I had picked up a book that taught basic Spanish. This probably sounds like a strange alternative to a possible presidential assassination, but I was getting edgy, afraid that it would become a reality, and was ready to try just about anything to avoid getting mixed up in something like that. While musing on these things, a police car drove up and two policemen got out, walking directly toward me. I wondered how I could have put myself in this situation, sitting in a park that winos frequented? But as the policemen got dangerously close, the pigeons suddenly flew away, and the officers handcuffed the wino and took him away. Breathing a sigh of relief, I got up to go home, just as a dusty van and two pickups pulled around the corner onto Lafayette Street. I could hear David Ferrie yelling orders in Spanish. "Andele, andele; vamanos!" I saw a dozen Cuban refugees dressed in a silly array of military clothing, loading heavy wooden boxes. Another bunch of hungry Cubans were heading for the lake. I walked on to Canal Street and took the first streetcar home.

The incident in the park was alarming to me. If I could just wait out the statute of limitations, I could eventually return to Oregon without ever being prosecuted for the bad checks my partner and I had written. The thought of returning to prison was something I just could not handle. The statute of limitations was up after three years, but I waited ten years before returning home to Oregon because of the short-term longevity of the witnesses who were connected to the assassination, and I was too afraid to come out of hiding.

In 1963 I wasn't sure what part the factions of the law, including local authorities, FBI, CIA, etc., played in the conspiracy, if they were active participants or merely gave silent consent. Knowing Banister had privy to any report to authorities, my life certainly would have been in danger by reporting to the wrong party, and this was my major fear. If you can't understand that, try putting yourself in my shoes.

I didn't have any friends in New Orleans except Lee, so I lived a lonely existence. It was so much different in Fort Worth, where I was surrounded by friends. As I have said, my lack of friends in New Orleans was the motive for my undivided friendship with Lee. In Fort Worth I would meet a friend who had a friend, and soon I would have lots of friends. Whereas in New Orleans I had only Lee and he had no other friends, so we both lived very lonely lives.

There were many things flashing through my mind as darkness fell on New Orleans that night. The revelations Lee shared with me added to my fear that I knew too much about the Walker case. If there was anything to what he had told me about the conspiracy, then surely I now knew more than it was healthy for me to know.

I became fearful that someone might be hiding outside my darkened window at night, so I turned off the lights as soon as darkness fell. I have never been able to discard the vision of General Walker, like a sitting duck in his brightly-lit study, with Lee pointing a rifle at his head. The vision was very intense because I had actually visited the General's house. As I lay in bed that sweltering August night, unable to sleep because of the stifling heat, I tried to evaluate the danger connected with Lee. I remembered him passing my apartment with the rifle in a makeshift package tucked under his arm, his silhouette darkened by the fading sun on the horizon. His head was bobbing and protruding forward, and he was taking funny, long strides like a cow. It was my impression that anyone with such idiosyncrasies could not be dangerous! I found myself smiling…yes, he was funny indeed. With that amusing thought in mind, I drifted off to sleep.

After the weekend had passed, and Monday morning rolled around, Lee was at the office bright and early to meet me, all excited about a great idea he had come up with. He could blow up the Huey Long Bridge! That would cause Mrs. Long to lose interest in politics by instilling in her such fear that she would be afraid to pursue her political interests. This would free me to help Lee hijack the plane, as there would no longer be a split in the Long political faction and Gillis would no longer need my help. He needed the hijacked plane to escape involvement in the assassination just as I was putting together my contingency plan to get out of town.

As serious as Lee was, I managed to shrug off his idea by trying to show him he didn't need any help with the plane, that it was possible to do it by himself. I didn't want any part of the plan so I said to him, "All you have to do, Lee, is go to Key West, take a small plane and persuade the pilot to take you to Havana." Then he could do whatever he wanted without involving me. When I mentioned to him that Cuba was only ninety miles from Key West he looked astonished, which surprised me since Lee fancied himself as a world traveler.

In her book, *Marina and Lee,* Priscilla McMillan stated that Lee mentioned Key West while measuring distances on his map. At one point he considered my suggestion about using the small plane, although he admitted that it didn't really fit his plans. He wanted a larger airliner, perhaps so it would give him a reason to involve me. But in looking at all the options, he obtained schedules from a smaller nearby airport which would have fewer passengers to subdue. He showed these to me, and upon reading the book, *Marina and Lee,* I found that he also showed them to Marina.

I continued to protest being involved in such a project, and after a couple of days Lee began to wear down on the subject. "Doesn't it bother you that they're planning to kill the president in there?" he asked. He was very convincing, and for the first time I began to put stock in what he was saying, but I made no effort to do anything about it.

My apathy at the time could have been connected with being incarcerated into an adult prison at a very young and impressionable age, or with my stay in Savannah where such threats were common. As for Lee, he seemed dejected and low in spirits because he knew the plan to kill the president was real. He was considered to be one of the participants in the assassination plot since he had gone out to the secret training base with David Ferrie to obtain marksmanship scores. Even if he deliberately got a less-than-perfect score, he was still a part of the plan and could not get out of it.

I made an effort to cheer him up and tried to get him to apply for a job at the packing house where I worked, which would offer him a new start. His spirits rose for a few moments while he considered it, but then in a voice filled with sadness, he said, "It's too late, Ron. I've done this to myself. I've messed up my life to where I can never be normal again. Everyone knows me and there is just too much publicity. It's too late."

The plan to kill the president was always on Lee's mind, and he wanted no part of it. No matter how hard I tried to convince him there was hope and that he could get out of it by leaving, it didn't seem to help. He said that wherever he moved to there would always be the threat of blackmail because of the Walker incident. There was also Marina and June to consider, since he loathed the idea of them being used as pawns. "You don't know these people like I do," he said. He felt there would be a threat over his family to keep him in check, and he feared that he could never shake the Banister apparatus. He felt if he could get his family back to Russia, they would be safe.

Our conversations were spaced out over several mornings. I can't remember exactly what was said on each specific day, although I do remember the content of what was said. At one point when the discussion turned to New York, I told Lee of my trip to Washington, D.C. and New York City. His ears perked up since he was considering the New York area as an alternate to Cuba at the time.

"I took a Greyhound to Washington, D.C. and New York while I was with the NAACP," I told Lee. "I got to the Big Apple on a Sunday morning, and it was certainly different from anything I'd ever seen. I've heard a lot about the city, but I never realized how awesome New York City really was!"

As Lee and I sat on the "chairs" in his office, he listened with great interest, as I continued. "The bus terminal was something like three stories below street level!" I explained, "So I got out and walked into the main lobby, and took an escalator up what seemed like three flights into the lobby on the street level."

I went on to relate to Lee the rest of what transpired during the trip. I was trying to figure out how to get to the street, when I saw in the distance a line of people about twelve or so abreast. I figured if I got in the line, it would take me there. I'm glad I never fell down, because I doubt if anyone would have bothered to help me up. If you could just manage to stay on your feet, you would make it to the street. Once I had reached it, it was necessary to cross it in order to get to a cab, which was a real challenge, because the street was so wide. It was the widest one I had ever seen and I had to get across it without getting hit by a car, which was no easy task. Darting in and out among traffic, with people honking and cursing at me, I finally made it to the cab and gave the driver the address of a hotel. It turned out to be only a couple of blocks away, and the fare was three-fifty, which I considered high in 1963.

I was at the hotel for about an hour when I decided to take a ride on a city bus so I could see the "Big Apple." After riding for hours I was still in the city! One of the passengers was listening to a baseball game on the radio, and a young couple was making out on one of the seats! "For God's sake!" I thought, disgusted. "Can't they even wait until they get off the bus?" New York City was already beginning to sicken me. I could hardly wait to get the hell out of there!

I got off the bus and walked two blocks to a neighborhood park, where people were lying around on towels and blankets, sunning themselves. They were packed like sardines in a can, and I couldn't see how it was humanly possible to cram another person into that congested area. However, People continued coming in droves and the first occupants kept scooting over, somehow making room for them. It was an incredible sight, that mass of humanity jammed so compactly together into such a small compound! Upon observing that squirming, multicolored conglomeration, I suddenly felt nauseated from the sight and smell of all that flesh.

I wasted no time finding the bus stop where I had disembarked, and in two hours I was back at the station. My suitcase wouldn't have been processed for another three days, but I spotted it after rummaging through three mountains of luggage, then I boarded the bus and headed for Savannah. It would take hours to get the city behind me. As the sun was setting and darkness fell, I looked through the rear window of the bus and saw the lights of New York city growing dim in the distance. By morning I was back in Savannah.

There was something in that account that interested Lee, and I never could figure out just what it was. But he told me that he had planned to go to the New York area as an alternate to Cuba. There were Russian communities there, which seemed to mean a lot to him. If they were to move there, however, it would mean that he and Marina would not be free from David Ferrie and Mr. Banister. "There's no friendship in this business," he said, "so be on your toes around David." The only way he could be free of them was to go to Cuba, where he could get back the self-esteem he lost when he returned to the United States. He would be something besides a messenger boy for Banister and would never have to stand in line for unemployment checks again.

"If I had to depend on thirty-three dollars a week, I couldn't even buy Marina a thirty-nine cent pair of panties," Lee told me. He discussed Marina's panties in his half-kidding, half-serious manner, saying, "I'm serious…you should see her panties! The elastic is giving out and she wants some new ones." He was laughing when he said this, and I laughed right along with him. Lee was such an intense person, and it was good to see him forget all else for a while and laugh at this very personal incident. I had seen Marina, and I knew she was several months pregnant. We weren't laughing at her condition, but the panties she wore obviously weren't designed for the latter stages of pregnancy. I chuckled as I visualized this, and I found it humorous.

Lee liked to pass on information, as he was a 007 type. He was pleased to be working for Mr. Banister, and was conscious of being promoted. He had already been upgraded from his job of locating left-wing students on the campus, to recruiting for Banister's various activities, such as my job at the Long rally. At this point he didn't know who he wanted to advance with, as he now had privy to the juiciest of all information…a plot to kill the president.

Early in September Lee decided to go to Washington to see the president. He said the assassination was scheduled to take place in Washington toward the end of September. "If that fails, it'll be in Texas," he said. On the basis of what I knew I wouldn't put stock in such a fairy tale, but Lee knew more than I did because he was a participant. Knowing he was deeper into that matter than I was, I didn't try to discourage him from going to Washington.

It was probably around the 5th or 6th that he had the most welcome news for me. Carefully emphasizing every word, he told me, "The assassination plan is a decoy." Lee was relieved that he hadn't gone to Washington. "The practice run is to route out any spies that might be in the woodwork." he said. "Just think, Ron. It almost brought out you and me." I didn't like the habit he had of including me in things he was involved in, such as the way I was drawn into the Clinton project. But that was just the way Lee was. It was difficult to be his friend without being involved.

Up until then, he had been trying to find someone he could tell about the assassination plan, and who could possibly do something about it. He was relieved to find out the plan was only a dry run, but he realized the next one would be the real thing. He continued to brood, and when I talked to him Friday morning, September 6th, he was hoping I would help him with the hijacking so he could pull out of the assassination plot. That weekend a climax would be reached in Lee's life.

There was a Rolando Cubella who met with a CIA case officer in 1961 in Brazil, and they were discussing a Castro assassination. They met again in September 1963, to continue their discussion. According to publications I've read…CIA headquarters received this information on September 7. The same day Castro happened to be at the Brazilian Embassy in Havana, making this statement: "United States leaders should think that if they are aiding terrorist plans to eliminate Cuban leaders, they would not be safe." I read about this in the *Times Picayune* newspaper on September 9. Even though Kennedy had suspended all attempts to assassinate Castro, the plan was moving ahead, and the agency was overruling a presidential order.

On Tuesday, September 10, I met with Lee at the regular place, and the first thing he asked was if I had read the article. I told him I had and at this time he began to drop the idea of hijacking a plane to Cuba. The plan began to take a back seat with Lee, and it was good news to me because there had been noticeable tension between us because of my unwillingness to drop everything and help him. I felt relieved as he began de-escalation of the hijacking plan, but knowing Lee as I did, I couldn't help but wonder what would be next.

I don't think I realized he had succumbed to the assassination plan. The message from Havana was a key factor in making his decision. My contingent plan to leave New Orleans was progressing since I had broken the ice with the girl named Elva in Harlengen, Texas. I knew Lee was hoping I would join him in Dallas, but I wasn't yet sure what I was going to do.

I had told David Ferrie I would call on him at his Parkway apartment, and on Sunday I decided to follow through. There were two things on my mind as I walked to his place. David was a homosexual and I needed to be prepared for any possible advances he might make. Also, there had been serious talk of assassinating the president, and the question entered my mind as I walked to his apartment, "What if he talks to me about the assassination, what should I do?" I had pretty much resolved that if David talked of killing Kennedy, I would go to the authorities. But I had the same concern Lee had...I didn't know who to trust. After all, Banister was the government, as much as the CIA and the FBI insist on denying that even to this day. I was afraid that whoever I contacted to expose the conspiracy, they would report it to Banister. Lee experienced these same feelings, and they were very intense!

In case David talked about the assassination, I was prepared to discuss it, but with the reservations that if I were given firsthand information in addition to what Lee had already told me, I might go to the local police. At that time I didn't even know what that might entail, and whether or not local authorities were involved in the plan. As it was, we didn't meet that day. I arrived at his apartment and knocked on the door, but didn't get an answer. I hoped he wasn't at home, but the place was unlocked, so I figured he had to be somewhere around. I opened the door and stepped inside. "David!" I called, but there was no response. A candle was still burning above the mantel where there were various colors of hardened, melted wax drippings that extended from the mantel onto the floor, probably accumulating from years of a ritualistic practice. It was an eerie sight, something you might expect to see in a horror movie! No wonder he wasn't afraid to leave the place unlocked, since the smell was enough to keep anyone out. There were mice cages everywhere, with hundreds of the little creatures scurrying back and forth in their cages. Some of them were dead. I remembered hearing that David was searching for a cure for cancer, so I presumed the mice were used in experiments of some kind. I nearly gagged as I quickly closed the door. If he ever questioned me about why I didn't come by, I could always tell him that I had stopped by but that he wasn't home.

MESSAGE FROM HAVANA

CHAPTER XI

On the way back to my place, I pondered over the article that had appeared in the local paper about Castro's willingness to eliminate American leaders. When I visited Banister's office, I'd noticed newspapers scattered about, and I had been told that Mrs. Roberts went over them with a fine-tooth comb as part of her job. That is how they first became interested in Gillis Long and how she had gotten the message from Havana.

Lee also received the signal, but probably with one slight difference. He heard only what he wanted to hear. He interpreted it in a way that allowed him to change his willingness to participate in the assassination plan developing at 544 Camp Street in New Orleans. The Banister apparatus and the Cuban refugees were no longer alone in their desire to see Kennedy eliminated. Now a prominent leader of a small but powerful and influential Caribbean nation was aligning himself with the Banister assassination conspiracy.

This signal had a lot of influence on Lee, and I have read books that expressed the author's curiosity as to how he might have reacted to Castro's statement that appeared in the New Orleans newspapers. I will probably be the only witness to ever tell of his reactions. The article disturbed him because he was dead-set against the assassination and had complained to me about it, but he didn't tell Banister. He just kept his feelings to himself but continued to confide in me, because I was his only confidant. He knew now that the message from Havana gave him new grounds to explore an involvement in the assassination conspiracy that was formulating. I saw the impression the article made on him from September 10 onward. Many things were then coming together in Lee's life, and it could have been to his advantage. But as we shall see, he would overcome one obstacle only to get himself into a worse situation, a trait that he expressed ever so often.

My next meeting with Lee was very satisfying. I was getting the impression that he had dropped the idea of the hijacking and the assassination of the Longs. Actually, it was more than just an impression. His life seemed to be moving in a good direction and this made me happy, because I wanted to go to Dallas with him as we had talked about on several occasions. However, I still had an alternate plan for going to Harlengen if he began to show any of his fatalistic traits again.

I told Lee of my contact with David Ferrie and Guy Banister at Katzenjammer's Bar, and also mentioned that I had gone to David's apartment and hadn't found him at home. He said it wasn't surprising, because there'd been some changes since we'd met at Katzenjammer's Bar.

Lee said, "David's now working with a client named Mr. Gill, who is an attorney. He's working on an assignment out of Gill's office in the Marquette Building, room 1707." He also said David could rarely be contacted there because he would be with the client, a tomato salesman. I questioned that, and he responded with that boyish grin on his face, "Yes, that's right, Ron, a tomato salesman."

We talked about Carlos Marcello, the Louisiana Mafia boss. It took me a while to realize that the tomato salesman and Carlos Marcello were one and the same. To put it mildly, Marcello had been deported in a very rude fashion by Attorney General Robert Kennedy, the president's brother. Without due process of law, Marcello was put on a plane and spirited off to a desolate part of Guatemala, where he almost died. Later, David Ferrie flew down to bring him back, which was illegal according to the Attorney General.

Marcello ironically won his case in court on November 22, 1963. The Marcello connection probably had a lot to do with Lee Harvey Oswald to a great degree, and it affected his life in a profound way. Lee said, "Don't underestimate Marcello, because he calls the shots here. It's his money we're using. He finances the Cuban projects." The thing that affected Lee most about Marcello, was that his attorney turned out to be Wray Gill, who was an associate of Russell Long. He soon learned that Russell was accepted by Banister, and realized that to kill him would be a big mistake.

Lee had been advocating the shooting of Mrs. Long and

the assassination of Senator Russell Long, but David's relationship with Wray Gill, the attorney working on the Marcello case, shed a new light in Lee's life. For at least a brief moment in Lee's fast-moving situation, things had finally started coming together.

Lee had noticed in an article in the August 22, 1963 edition of *The Times Picayune* newspaper in New Orleans, that Senator Long had made a stand against Martin Luther King's march on Washington. Long stated in the article, entitled "Long Doubtful on Pack Stand," that if the march were conducted in an orderly manner it could be helpful, but if it got out of hand, it would hurt their cause. He said he was against the civil rights legislation asked by Kennedy, and that he just as soon the whole thing broke out in riots.

This article was typical of what fueled Lee's hatred of Russell Long, because Lee favored the civil rights bill. Regardless of the reasons he used to justify killing the senator, Lee was still able to overcome his desire to take action. Carlos Marcello, a powerful Mafia leader who threatened to kill Kennedy, was a Banister client and a comrade of David Ferrie. Lastly, Marcello's attorney, Wray Gill, was an associate of Russell Long, which I explicitly remember Lee telling me. This association was profound enough to save Russell's life, which was good news to me, because I could have been implicated, had the plan moved forward.

Lee was capable of gratitude, as shown when he shook my hand and said, "Thanks for your resistance, Ron. Sometimes I get carried away." He was referring to his proposition to assassinate Russell Long and hijack a plane to Cuba. He no longer needed the plane, but I didn't understand why at the time. For some reason Lee had joined the assassination plan with the Banister apparatus. It seemed Castro was now aligned with the conspiracy and Lee was attracted to the assassination, but I wasn't aware of it at the time, so I slept well at night.

It would have been foolish for Lee to kill Senator Long at that particular time, even though the Senator had been detrimental to Congressman Gillis Long's campaign for governor of Louisiana, and was critical of Kennedy's civil rights bill. If Lee had killed the Senator, he never would have lived to see Kennedy assassinated, which was eventually important to him.

Lee was aware of the Louisiana gubernatorial race, and as it progressed to full-swing, he became aware that there was a Kennedy and an anti-Kennedy faction, which was an issue in the election. Lee and I discussed this many times, and I believe the Kennedy faction was just one of the determining factors that led him to participate in the assassination. The president's death would force the candidates to deal with the real issues in the campaign, rather than who was for Kennedy and who was against him, and this was disgusting to Lee.

In retrospect, the *States Item,* a New Orleans newspaper, alluded to this in the November 30, 1963 edition, under the article entitled, "Kennedy's Death Destroys Top Issue in Gubernatorial Campaign." There is no doubt in my mind that the Banister cronies pointed out to Lee that Castro was now aligned with them. I am sure they felt the president's death would result in the gubernatorial candidates dealing with issues such as automation, Lee's pet peeve, rather than who Kennedy was or was not backing. Long would benefit by Kennedy's death, and would no longer be handicapped, since he had resisted various attempts to have him join the anti-

Kennedy chorus echoing within Louisiana.

Lee preferred to deal with people who believed in their causes. Even though he couldn't be trusted, his relations with David Ferrie and me seemed to indicate that he believed in his causes also, just as we did. He resisted Banister's plan of assassination until he had sufficient cause to join them, and I believe Lee needed a reason for his involvements. I wondered if perhaps he needed a grudge to pique his interest in assassinations, or if something else was required.

If it's true, as I suspect, that Lee needed a motive for participating, he now had an assortment of incentives before him from which to choose. Castro was now aligned with Banister's plan to kill the president, and the assassination would remove one obstacle from in front of Gillis Long, because he refused to join the anti-Kennedy chorus.

It was evident that there was a change in Lee from that point on. It isn't easy to judge just what event or circumstances whetted his appetite for the adventure and intrigue connected with assassinations. What was behind his changeover to the Banister plan? The real motive may have been concealed, but certainly his behavior betrayed his masquerade by the fact that he didn't advocate the hijacking plan anymore, and was no longer trying to devise ways to get out of it.

Occasionally, Lee expressed amazement over some event he was involved in...for instance, when he made this statement: "I met with Maurice Bishop in Dallas yesterday at a skyscraper called the Southland Center. Bishop's not his real name, but at least, I've finally met the head of Alpha 66!" Lee was amazed that he had been sent on that mission. He wouldn't have made a very good spy, because he usually gave himself away, although he was learning the spy business better every day.

There are a couple of things I want to mention that Lee and I discussed during the months I was associated with him. One thing is that he told me of going to an attorney, Dean Andrews, to get the status of his undesirable discharge changed. Since I also had one I would like to have upgraded, I said, "How much did the guy charge you?"

"Nothing," he replied. "At the point where I had to come up with money, I just got up and walked out."

"Without a word?" I asked. He replied laughingly, "Without a word." To my knowledge, he never went back nor did anything more in the interest of getting his discharge upgraded. Lee never got angry nor made immoral gestures, at least not in my presence. He would often just walk away when irritated, or sometimes he would just laugh.

Around the middle of September Lee told me, "I'm going to be moving to Dallas soon. You're welcome to go with me, if you want to." I listened carefully, because now he was beginning to show some common sense. As I've said, he was glad he hadn't shot Russell or Mrs. Long. Russell was practically a part of the Banister apparatus since Mr. Gill came into the picture, and Lee had even expressed gratitude for my resistance to his hijacking plan. Yes, Lee was capable of showing gratitude.

I considered going with him to Dallas, but I would be watching closely for his old traits to resurface. I never did tell him of my alternate plan to go to Harlengen if the need arose, which did eventually turn out to be the case.

Lee told me he was driven to Dallas by private auto. "A guy named Frank took me," he said.

"Was he a Cuban?" I asked.

"No, he was a gringo," he answered.

I remembered the name, because I associated it with the Frank I knew in Fort Smith, Arkansas. It is commonly believed that a man named Frank Sturgis drove Lee to Dallas, and I believe this to be the case. This was one of the times he expressed amazement that he had been chosen to go on that secret mission. I asked him why he had been chosen and he answered, puzzled-like, "I don't know." However, he showed his elation about being privileged to go on such a 007 rendezvous.

By this time Lee was learning to use discretion, to keep quiet about certain things, especially about his involvement with the plot to kill the president. Marina liked Kennedy, and Lee had learned from the Walker incident to keep his mouth shut when it came to shooting people. I liked Kennedy too, and Lee was well aware of this. The only reason I had for believing he was involved was that he no longer made any move to withdraw from any connection to the assassination from that point on. This was a complete about-face from his attitude two weeks before.

Because of the subsequent assassination, this was doubtless a focal point of the Bishop meeting. However, Lee never mentioned anything to me of an impending Mexican venture. It seemed that he never knew his schedule until it was time for action, and I usually found out about his exploits after the fact. I felt sure he wasn't deliberately keeping things from me, as Lee shared practically everything with me. I'm certain it was the fact that he didn't know his schedule in advance that kept me from knowing things ahead of time, such as his trip to Mexico. I think they "sprang" things on him.

I had heard very little of the planned assassination since September 10 and I was breathing a little easier, although it proved to be only a lull in the storm. I didn't know Lee was going to be out of town the day he went to Dallas to meet with Maurice Bishop. I went to his office at the Crescent City Garage and was waiting for him on the foundation we always sat on. It was already close to 8:00 A.M. when I began to wonder if this was going to be one of the days that Lee wouldn't show up at all. At that moment a young man came into the office and stood before me. He announced, "Hi, Ron; I'm Lee Oswald. Remember me?" He remained standing instead of sitting, as Lee always did.

I was startled and alarmed! In the first place, it wasn't Lee, and I didn't want to deal with anyone but Lee ever since I heard of the assassination plan. I thought the wisest thing to do was to say, "Hi, Lee, what's up?" to make him think I believed him, and it worked. I was afraid it wouldn't, because I knew Lee so intimately, but he obviously didn't realize this. I didn't know if I would be able to put on a good enough act to fool him.

"Just taking a breather," he answered, "It's hot as hell in the office."

"It's not nine yet; how can that be?" I asked.

"There's all kinds of heat, Ron," he answered. I knew what he meant, so I didn't comment any further. I never did tell Lee about the incident, but maybe I should have, and perhaps he could have filled me in on the details. At that particular time I was trying to keep things around me as low-profile as possible, so I said nothing about it.

The man was young, about Lee's age, and was clean-shaven, with a slight stocky build, a lot like Lee. But I could tell the difference, because his hip swung to the right, and Lee never stood like that. After a few words he excused himself and left, something Lee had never done. I would always be the one who left first when one of our meetings ended. Over the years, I tried numerous times to figure out the identity of the man, and what his motivation was. I wondered if it might have been the man who had impersonated Lee on several occasions, setting him up as a patsy. Because I was acquainted with Lee, I figured they tested him out on me, hoping he was a good enough impersonator to fool me into thinking he was Lee.

As I thought about that particular incident many times throughout the years, I remembered distinctly how the guy looked, and he just didn't resemble Lee that much. For one thing, his chin was somewhat square and wide, where Lee's chin was rather pointed. Also, when he stood erect, his right hip shifted to the right and slightly forward. I wanted very much to believe I had solved the mystery so that I could put it out of my mind. Consequently, I made myself believe that the man in question was the original imposter. However, in 1990 I saw a picture of him in the newspaper, and learned that his name was Roscoe White. I recognized the face immediately as the man who had confronted me in Lee's office in 1963. I couldn't believe it! After more than a quarter of a century, I had finally found out his identity and it was Rosoe White, the man Lee told me was being trained to kill President Kennedy! The features were identical to the man I had met at the Crescent City Garage.

I was familiar with Roscoe's name in 1963, although I never met him under that name, but under the name of Lee Oswald. I'm not going to try to figure out the reason for the impersonation, but I am going to emphatically state that it was Roscoe White I met that day, posing as Lee. Someday perhaps we'll know the reason for the pretense, as the remaining pieces of the puzzle are put together.

I was beginning to hope the assassination plan was about to dissipate, because Lee wasn't grumbling about it anymore. But on September 17, I realized something was still in the wind. Lee told me there was a man named Joseph Kramer staying at the Royal Orleans Hotel, who had recently become one of Banister's employees. Kramer, a CIA agent who was loyal to the president, had sent his superiors information that an assassination was scheduled to take place September 26 in Washington, D.C. The decoy plan worked, and a spy was routed out of the woodwork. Lee knew of the plans, and he was now engaged in the implementation of the November 22 plan that would be employed in Dallas.

Daily, I would receive updates on the elusive Mr. Kramer, which showed that Lee was a very informed person at the center of the Banister apparatus. Surely, he was a more important person to those he was involved with than history has given him credit for. Around the 22nd Lee told me, "Banister had me steal a drinking glass out of Kramer's room. It went without a hitch. They found his prints on the glass, and the guy's name is really Richard Filmore." This is now a well-known fact, but it's interesting to note that Lee was actually involved in the action.

In his desperation to get away from Banister and put himself in the hands of local police, Kramer walked into a bank in El Paso, fired two shots into the ceiling, and yelled, "This is a stickup!" then sat down and waited to be arrested. Banister, learning of the incident within minutes, roared, "The asshole fell right into our hands. He held up a Federal Reserve bank! We'll have him behind bars forever where he can't talk!"

Marina and Lee weren't getting along too well at that time. It wasn't that Lee told me about this in no uncertain terms, but it was just that his behavior betrayed him. Marina was about to leave for Irving, a Dallas suburb, to stay with her friend, Mrs. Payne. This seems to have been part of the overall plan, but it was a charade that Lee wasn't overjoyed about. He was critical of Marina's friends and believed Mrs. Payne was trying to break them up.

Lee used his petty jealousies to put the blame on his favorite competition for the problems in his marriage, rather than on his own shortcomings. He was always jealous of Marina's Russian friends who lived in Dallas, and would subconsciously blame them for his inability to live with her and at the same time play the 007.

On September 24 Lee told me, "I'm a bachelor now, just like you. I can leave the house anytime I want." But he never changed his habits. He continued to meet me early in the morning and was always home by sundown. In fact, he told me that when he passed my house with the rifle in August, he was home before dark.

Marina left for Dallas on the 23rd of September, and on the 24th, Lee had already begun to miss her. He again talked of going to Dallas. "I'm going over there to get Marina back. Wanna' come with me, Ron?" he asked. But I declined because of the Gillis Long rallies. Lee accepted that excuse better than I thought he would. He said he respected me for sticking with my candidate and not deserting him.

One reason why I believe Lee didn't necessarily know of his assignments in advance was that if he had known he was going to Mexico or any place other than Dallas, he wouldn't have invited me to go with him. It's a well-known fact that he went to Mexico City upon leaving New Orleans. I met with him on September 24th and again on the 25th, and he didn't mention anything about going to Mexico. This was no doubt because he thought he was going to Dallas.

Having met with Marina in December 1990, I found she knew of his Mexico trip in advance, which concerned me. "Yes, Lee told me before he left that he was going to Mexico," she said. He seldom kept information from me, but if he did hold anything back, that meant his business was doubtless connected to the assassination plot. If that were the case he knew I wouldn't approve and that I might expose him, so it's understandable why he wouldn't have confided in me about the trip.

I'll admit that Marina's claim that she knew about it in advance lends weight to the theory that he held back the information from me. I will later tell of a meeting we had after his return, which may give some insight into why he apparently didn't want me to know he was going to Mexico.

I met with Lee again on September 25, the day he left New Orleans. As usual, it was about 7:00 A.M., and he said he had come to pick up his unemployment check. The post office didn't open until 9:00 o'clock. He told me, "I stayed at my apartment last night, even though I owe rent." The rent was owed because the landlord was at fault for something or other, and Lee felt justified in not paying it. As I recall, the reason seemed valid to me, but I can't remember the nature of the conflict.

"I went to the bus depot yesterday evening and rented a security box to put my luggage in," Lee informed me. "I didn't want my landlord to know I was leaving, so I had to brave the dark to get my luggage there without being seen, since I planned to leave early this morning."

He told me again that he had been afraid of the dark ever since his Marine Corp buddy was killed, and that there were some people who believed he was responsible for his death.

"Well are you?" I asked, remembering the first conversation Lee and I had about Martin Schrand, and how I had tried to get him to say whether or not he had killed him.

"It was an accident," he said, quietly.

I've never been able to determine just what he meant by that answer, whether he was involved or not, but he did say he wasn't responsible.

Lee left his house on the morning of the 25th and went to his office, just an indenture off the street where he found a measure of security, a refuge from the world. At that meeting he expressed sadness for the way his life was turning out. "I know another road would've led to a more peaceful role in life," he told me. If I had been able to read between the lines, I could have sensed he was going on a mission of some sort, instead of to Dallas to get his wife back. However, one thing I'm certain of is that he was not leaving for Cuba, and had no intentions of going there, as this narration will later reveal.

Lee tried to ease my mind in connection with the plans to kill the president. "I'll speak to Kennedy when I get to Dallas," he reassured me, but I knew he wouldn't be able to accomplish that. "Lee, there are thousands of people wanting to talk to the president, and you think you can get to him?" I questioned.

"Yes, I have a plan to warn the president," he responded. I knew in my heart that was impossible, and I felt it was as though he had compromised his former position of resisting the assassination plan. But Lee didn't want to discuss it any further, so his conversation took a new slant. He began to talk of his family, whom he already missed terribly. He spoke of how he used to play a horse race game at the amusement park at Lake Pontchartrain. He said he had always won and would use his winnings to buy hamburgers for Marina and June.

I left for work about 7:45 A.M., so I spent approximately forty-five minutes in conversation with him the morning he left. I knew he was scheduled to be on the noon bus heading out of New Orleans later that day. That evening on my way home I walked by the office and Lee wasn't there, indicating that he had left on the noon bus as scheduled.

History depicts Lee as being a loner, a nut, a man who confided in no one, but Lee was anything but that kind of person. He had a deep need to confide in someone. It was just as necessary to him as physical food. He did have a fatalistic side and as I've said before, the person he confided in would have to serve as his monitor to keep him from performing self-destructive acts that he was unable to control. Without such a person he was a doomed man, and there was no one that could even attempt to fill the bill from that point on, except perhaps Marina.

History doesn't record the human side of Lee, his urges to destroy and his fight to resist those urges. This document, however, discusses an era in the life of the man accused of killing the president. These things have never before been related, and they must be given credibility in order to establish a record that portrays some of his more intimate dealings rather than the intrigue that is now attributed to him. He wasn't an elusive and shadowy figure, as this narration shows, but was a genuine human being with the needs and emotions of any other human.

When Lee left New Orleans there is some controversy as to where he went while on his way to Mexico. On the day he left, he told me he hadn't shaved since Marina left on the 23rd, which would be his third day without shaving. There's a record that indicates he went to see the governor in Austin, but I'm going to discount that as either a forgery, or perhaps an error of some kind, since the Odio incident sounds more realistic to me. I wouldn't have even noticed that Lee hadn't shaved, but he brought it to my attention on the 25th. He apologized for not having shaved, and this is how I know he left unshaven. The visitor that Sylvia Odio, of Dallas, had on the night of the 25th, the man that she said was Lee, was not shaven, and of course, I'm going to give that story some credibility. She said the visitor who resembled Lee that came to see her on the night of September 25, was unshaven.

The fact that he was in the company of two Latins proves that he wasn't alone in this scenario, and this tells me that someone else was behind the trip. I feel that without any doubt whatsoever, it was Guy Banister and his elements. Lee left for Mexico City right after the meeting with Odio, and I had no further contact with him until October 11.

LEE WITHOUT A MENTOR

CHAPTER XII

It is a known fact that George de Mohrenchildt served as Lee's mentor in 1962, and his unwitting encouragement may have led to the Walker incident. To be Lee's ideal friend was a complicated matter because one had to serve as friend, mentor and constituent. De Mohrenchildt fit into only two of these categories, as he was only Lee's friend and mentor, and not his constituent. Instead, Lee was devoted to him, which was not an ideal situation. De Mohrenchildt likened Walker to Adolf Hitler because of his fascism. Lee told Marina after the Walker incident, "Walker's a good deal like Hitler, and if Hitler had been stopped by an assassin's bullet before his escapades, the world would've been better off." (10) De Mohrenchildt had some commendable traits, as he started The National Foundation for Cystic Fibrosis. Incidentally, Jacqueline Kennedy was appointed as honorary chairman for the organization.

In New Orleans I served as Lee's mentor, but discouraged him from violent acts and was barely able to provide him with resistance. Now that he was in Dallas and George was in Haiti, Lee would be without a mentor, and what was worse he had fallen into the hands of conspirators. Of course, I didn't know he had gone to Mexico. I was just enjoying his absence. Being Lee's friend involved commitment and obligation, and included participation in his involvements. Dealing with his complex personality involved constant pressure and uncertainties because of his interests.

Going to Dallas with Lee was still on my list of alternatives, because I was planning on leaving New Orleans after the December 7 state elections. My contingent plan to go to Harlengen was progressing. I still wasn't certain where I would go, but a lot depended on Lee, and whether or not he could stay out of trouble long enough for me to regain confidence in him.

At this point I will provide background information for certain things I had hoped to conceal about the October 11 meeting. It's not because of any feeling of complicity on my part, but because I have always been sensitive about this one incident. I was apprehensive because I felt I knew too much about Lee's life and the impending assassination, so I turned off the lights in the apartment early at night. I was afraid Lee or someone at 544 Camp Street, might decide to take a shot at me, and I was worried.

During the first part of October, Lee was involved in the plan to kill the president, and was meeting frequently with Ruby. He had violated the trust of the Banister apparatus by telling me of the impending assassination, and he was worried about it. He hadn't talked to me since September 25 and was no doubt uneasy, perhaps wondering, "Has Ron gone to the authorities in my absence?"

Lee planned to go to New Orleans on October 11, and he needed an ingenious plan that would provide him with an alibi to prove he had never been away from Dallas. If he got the gut feeling after talking to me that he couldn't trust me, he wouldn't hesitate to kill me, friend or no friend. Likewise, if word leaked out about the assassination plan and Lee was the source of the leak, he and his family would suffer for it. So in his eyes, it was necessary for him to return to New Orleans so that he could size up the situation.

He drew up a plan out of one of the James Bond books he'd been reading, and told his landlady Mrs. Bledsoe, "I'm gonna be in my room reading all day Friday and I don't want to be disturbed." He slipped quietly out his bedroom window on the second story and proceeded with his 007 plan. I remember him telling me it was on the second floor and that he had a way of getting to the ground and back again in an easy manner. He never told me how he did it, but I visualized him utilizing a tree in the process, although I never asked him about it.

In 1991 I visited the site at 621 North Marsalis, where Lee lived at Mrs. Bledsoe's rooming house for the first week after he went back to Dallas, but the house had been torn down. However, the tree that was still standing appeared to be close enough to where the structure was situated, that it could have been the one Lee talked about climbing down when he sneaked out of his room on October 11, 1963. Information acquired through later research brings the address into question, as the house could have been located at 603 North Marsalis. Lee told me he lived upstairs in Mrs. Bledsoe's house, which was in an area of nothing but two-story houses. When Larry Howard and I visited the site of 621, I remember him saying, "Well, they are all two-story houses, so this could be the site."

I used to chide Lee about reading fiction. When he came back to see me on October 11 he told me about coming up with his clever plan to go to New Orleans. "I prepared my alibi out of one of my James Bond novels," he told me, somewhat smugly. "You see, this is why I read them. Wasn't that plan ingenious?"

On October 11, which was a Friday, Lee and I went into the indenture and sat down on the "chairs." I am sure of the date, because it was ironically my last day of work at the meat plant. After talking to Lee about the election and other small matters, he announced, "I'm confident I won't have to kill you, Ron, because I feel I've still got your loyalty."

Suddenly, my world grew smaller as my mind zeroed in on my surroundings. Lee and I were alone in his office at 7:30 in the morning with no one else around, and here he was…my best friend…talking about killing me! I started feeling a little queasy and my hands began to tremble. It felt stuffy and I found it hard to breathe. I suddenly had the urge to rush outside to get some fresh air! It reminded me of the time I sat in the gas chamber when I was in prison.

The streets were empty, and there were no signs of activity; none of the normal, everyday things like a mechanic working on a car, or someone changing a tire. At that particular moment, I was beginning to feel quite apprehensive. I knew I had a lot of influence with Lee, even though he'd talked of killing me. If that was still on his mind, maybe I could talk him out of it. True, he'd said he felt he still had my loyalty, and was sure he wouldn't have to kill me, but there was always the possibility.

The big question in my mind was…where was his pistol? Lee, quick to read my mind, said, "I know what you're thinking, Ron. Don't be alarmed; I don't have my pistol with me. I was afraid I might be searched, so I couldn't carry it across the state line on the bus. But I could kill you in a second and you know that." Lee may have actually had no intention of killing me. He may have only been trying to impress upon me the seriousness of the situation. However, I realized he meant business! Either the days were getting darker, as it was mid-October, or else fright just has a way of making things seem darker. Martin Schrand stood out clearly in my mind at that moment! Was there a possibility he had known too much about the dark side of Lee Oswald?

I was afraid the thing I dreaded had come to pass. I realized that if the things I had been told were true, there was no hope for the president. If I wanted to live, I would just keep my mouth shut and hope for the best from then on. Perhaps I had been programmed in prison to play my cards close to the chest and worry about my own circumstances.

It seemed evident that Lee had joined the conspirators in their plot to assassinate Kennedy! My main concern at that moment was to save my own life, and in order to do this, I used all of the influence and expertise I had accumulated as one of Banister's men. It was similar to the story of the Lone

Ranger and Tonto, when surrounded by an enormous crowd of Indians. The Lone Ranger said, "What will we do now, Tonto?" And Tonto replied, "What do you mean *we*, White man?" For now, I was one of Banister's men!

"Of course you could kill me, Lee," I agreed. "We're in a risky business…we both know that. It's because you go beyond the rules set by Banister that you get yourself in trouble. Take Senator Long, for instance. What if you had taken him out without consulting Guy? Right now, you'd be a dead man! Yes, you owe me, Lee, and you've got to learn to play by the rules."

Lee replied, "I came here knowing that I may have to kill you Ron, and you have to admit that if that turned out to be necessary, no one could connect me with the crime. You don't have any I.D., and these winos die around here all the time, and no one will ever know I was in New Orleans today. But I'm convinced you haven't told anyone about the assassination, and anyway, you know what problems Joe Kramer had because he decided to talk. I don't think you'll forget you're a fugitive, and besides, no one really knows for sure what's going to go down, so you can rest on that count."

This is the issue that I almost concealed. The reason I didn't want to tell about it wasn't because Lee had used stronger language with me about the assassination, but it was because I was ashamed he had talked about killing me.

It was at this meeting that I learned several things about Lee's Mexican venture. On the bus trip to Mexico City, there was a CIA agent seated next to him. He was aware the man was an agent, but we determined in our discussion that he had no connection with the scenario that was taking place. Lee arrived in Mexico City September 27, 1963, carrying two suitcases that he had put in the security box in New Orleans. This was alluded to in a preceding chapter.

When Lee left New Orleans on September 25, he told me he would have a new contact, Jack Ruby, a man he was acquainted with, and said he would be meeting him in Dallas on October 5. Lee didn't tell me he was going to Mexico, so I thought he was going to Dallas.

My last visit with Lee was on October 11, eight days after he had returned to Dallas from Mexico. He met his new contact, Jack Ruby, as scheduled, and Ruby was to help him get a job in Dallas as well as aiding him in other areas, such as finding a place to stay and introducing him to new friends. Incidentally, the situation with Ruby was much the same as it was with George de Mohrenchildt.

The Banister apparatus was not the moving party behind the assassination, but they were deeply involved. Today, I doubt that the Cuban government was a prime instigator of the assassination, but Cuba was an important ingredient, as their approval meant a lot to Lee and to the prime movers, as well as to Banister. In a maneuver of this magnitude it was necessary for all allies to stick together.

Lee took a Cubana Airlines flight from Mexico City to Ontario, Canada, accompanied by a CIA agent who was more prominent than Banister, one with a more direct connection to the government. It was probably David Phillips or perhaps someone ordered by Phillips, to accompany Lee. At any rate, someone from Mexico City went with Lee, but where that person came from or how he got to the city, I have forgotten. Lee and that individual flew to Canada and turned around and flew directly back, this much I am absolutely positive of. Based on our conversation, I believe with good cause that these parties met with a Cuban in Canada, whom I believe was Che Guevera.

Lee was involved at that time in the plans to assassinate Kennedy, and this was discussed at the Ontario meeting. Because of the subsequent assassination, it wouldn't be logical to think that Lee was discussing anything but this at that particular time. David Phillips was a CIA officer who worked in Mexico City at the time Lee visited there, and I believe he was the mysterious Maurice Bishop, head of Alpha 66.

A short time after Lee and the agent arrived back in Mexico City, Lee went by bus to Dallas. According to information I had received, he met with Jack Ruby on October 5, and I can't recall him telling me of the full content of that meeting. He no doubt had more dealings than I am relating, but I can only relate what I know to be factual. The following conversation between Lee and Ruby is based on what Lee told me.

"Did you meet the Cuban in Ontario?" Ruby asked Lee.

"Yeah, I met the egghead," Lee replied.

"Why do you call him that?" Ruby asked. "We're all in this together."

"Well, Jack," Lee replied, "You'd think he was acting under orders from Fidel, but it's a situation like the relationship between Kennedy and the CIA. Castro doesn't know."

"Well, I'll be damned," said Ruby, "this is a new twist. We were under the impression we were dealing with Castro because of his alignment statement."

"You'd better call Guy and tell him it's not Castro we're dealing with; it's Che Guevera," Lee said.

Looking back on the situation, I've always wondered why Castro fired Guevera. Was it the assassination that caused the rift between them?

That particular meeting with Lee was the October 11 meeting I referred to earlier. I was on my way to work when we met, and we talked for more than an hour. After discussing some developments in the election, he asked me to fill out the change-of-address card for him which he already had on his person. This indicated to me that even before he left Dallas, he had planned to have me fill it out for him when he got to New Orleans. Perhaps this was one reason he made the 500-mile trip. I hesitated because I just didn't want to take a chance of having my handwriting on anything, but Lee insisted, so I printed his Magazine Street address on the form, as well as his new address in Irving, where Marina was staying. I asked him how to spell "Magazine," since I didn't know if it had a "z" or an "s" in it. Lee felt confident that it was a "z." "After all, I lived on Magazine Street," he told me.

When Lee came to New Orleans on October 11, he asked me again to go to Dallas, but I used the election as an excuse for not going at that time, and it wouldn't be over until December 7. Just like before, he accepted the reason I gave him without any argument, but he did give his address to me, which he wrote down on a scrap of paper that I tore from my lunch bag. I don't remember for sure, but it's possible he wrote down the phone number on it also. I kept the paper in my possession until November 24. "You can always find me through the Irving address," Lee told me. "Watch the papers also, since you might be reading about me, and you'll be able to find me that way," He didn't give me any indication that he planned to be in jail. I strongly felt that Lee planned to turn the tables on the Banister apparatus, so they would be the ones in the hot seat instead of him. This is also an indication that he didn't pull the trigger that killed the president. But regardless of who did, Lee did not plan on going to jail, at least not for long.

One thing for sure, though, the gubernatorial campaign wasn't going well for Gillis. He wasn't out of the race, but he simply wasn't in the leading position. Lee and I discussed the fact that Gillis had refused to join the anti-Kennedy chorus, and his middle-of-the-road tactics weren't acting in his favor at the time. He needed help more than ever!

I had knocked on a lot of doors, handing out particulars, and I wanted to continue doing so. Lee commended me for not deserting Gillis. He told me, "You can expect a change in the Gillis Long status before the upcoming election, Ron,...one that should put him in a more favorable light." Lee had been quite concerned about Gillis' refusal to join the anti-Kennedy chorus, which was costing him votes in Louisiana. He was happy about the refusal, but concerned about the loss of popularity because of it. However, Lee no longer expressed his former concern about that particular situation, and it is noteworthy that he once was worried about it.

I was pleased that Lee was no longer pressing for a local assassination as he had previously. This was good news to me, and this fact more than anything else, could possibly persuade me to actually go to Dallas after the election. I knew he had some political ambitions he was holding back from me, because of his statement that I might be reading about him in the newspaper. He also mentioned that he would be renting an apartment Ruby had found for him at 1026 N. Beckly Street, and he'd kept his appointment with Ruby as scheduled. When we came to the subject of work, Lee told me he already had a job secured at the Texas School Book Depository. That was on a Friday, and was ironically, my last day at work. I was always concerned about getting a job, because I depended on it in order to survive, and had no one to fall back on in case I went through a period of unemployment.

"Are you really certain about getting the job at the Texas School Book Depository?" I asked Lee. The name of the place was impressive, so it stayed with me.

"It's a sure thing, Ron; there's no way that job can fall through!" he answered. I want to emphasize the fact that he made that statement on October 11, three days before he was supposed to have even known about the job, according to historical records.

I told Lee I had been studying Spanish and he said, "Heck, if I would have known that, you could have gone to Mexico with me. Anyhow, I didn't stay in Mexico all that long. We took a Cubana Airlines flight to Ontario." By what Lee told me during our conversation, I assumed he took the trip alone, but he assured me there was a man accompanying him. I thought he said it was the same man he met at the Southland Center, but I am not absolutely certain.

Before I left for work that day, Lee asked me to do him a favor. "Ron," he said, "I need you to fill out this change-of-address card and go to the post office across Lafayette Square and drop it in the letter box."

"How come you want me to do that, Lee?" I asked.

"I'm afraid someone will recognize me if I do it, then Carlos would find out I've been here," he answered. He wanted to keep his trip to New Orleans a secret. He had mentioned Carlos several times before, but I wouldn't remember his name again until 1965 when I met another man named Carlos, who would bring it back to mind.

"Man, I can't, Lee, I'm scared of the Square," I objected.

"What's your problem now, Ron?" he questioned.

"Well, I saw a wino get arrested there, actually handcuffed and taken away by the cops," I told him.

"You can't get arrested in Lafayette Square," he said, "You must've been mistaken. It's impossible to get arrested in the Square. Just look around," he said, confidently, "Over there's the CIA, in the federal building. You know we load and un-load Cubans and weapons all the time right in front of Banister's office. This part of town is protected by diplomatic immunity."

"You mean I didn't see a wino get arrested?" I asked, knowing perfectly well what I'd seen.

"That's right, Ron. You were mistaken," he answered. "If you're ever in trouble with the police, just hide in Lafayette Square and you'll be safe. What you saw was something clandestine...maybe one of the Washington boys playing the wino, and he saw too much. That guy's probably dead by now."

I hesitantly took the change-of-address card, walked across Camp Street to the post office, and dropped it in the mailbox. Then I waived "goodbye" to Lee and headed for work, never to see him again. As I went to bed that night, I could visualize him sneaking into Mrs. Bledsoe's rooming house by way of his bedroom window, giving the appearance that he had been in his room all day.

I had to work Saturdays at my new job, but on the first Sunday after I started working, I walked all the way down Ca-nal Street just to kill time, then went over to 544 Camp Street. Everything looked the same, but I still had no friends. Lee was gone and Mr. Banister's office was closed up tighter than a drum, so I just milled around in the area of Lafayette Square, then returned to my apartment. In less than a month President Kennedy would be dead, and two days later, Lee would be dead also.

Between Lee's October 11 visit and the assassination, I worked six days a week in the store, and in the meantime I began changing my lifestyle. I bought some Western boots, a rugged Western coat and a Stetson hat. Sometimes in the cool of the evening I would venture out to a bar, order a beer and listen to Western music. One night in October after Lee had left for Dallas, I was listening to the radio while a car lot conducted a sell-a-thon. I recognized the name of the dealership ...Stephens Chevrolet, as the one Jack Lawrence had been associated with. He was the man Lee and I had discussed previously. I listened closely for the address, 840 Carondelet. I got out my city map, checking to see if it was within walking distance.

After giving it some thought, I figured I could probably nose around the car lot and find out something about the assassination, to corroborate what Lee had told me. Thus I probably hold the title of the world's first assassination researcher. I hung around a bit, but purposely wore the cowboy outfit so I wouldn't be recognized as a Banister associate. The disc jockey singled me out, asking if I had a horse to trade in. I could see that he was determined to bring me up in front of the crowd that had assembled, and I might possibly be recognized. I had been told to steer clear of this place, so I made a quick exit before that could happen. As I left the dealership, I could hear the disc jockey talking about the cowboy who wanted to trade in his horse for a car. I have a feeling that was a popular topic of conversation around the place for days.

Research shows that a Jack Lawrence worked at a downtown Dallas Lincoln-Mercury dealership, which had loaned cars for the presidential motorcade. At the time of the assassination Lawrence had worked there a month. Everyone in America could remember where they were and what they were doing the moment Kennedy was shot, but Lawrence couldn't account for his time. It was "recalled that thirty minutes after the assassination, Lawrence, muddy and sweating profusely, came running into the dealership and was overcome by nausea. His abandoned vehicle was later found parked behind the picket fence on the grassy knoll. Jack Lawrence was arrested later that afternoon, and held in jail for twenty-four hours." (11)

Events that stand out in my memory from the time Lee left to the assassination, was a hurricane that ventured close to New Orleans and a number of local twisters that upturned cars and wrecked several buildings. I remember wearing my heavy coat, expecting strong winds that never came, except for those that were brought on by a few outlying twisters.

On November 22 I had just gotten settled at my new job. In order to get there, it was necessary to take the streetcar down Canal Street for a short distance, then transfer to a bus. I did not want my employer to know I traveled by bus, nor where I came from, so I got off two blocks from the neighborhood store where I worked and walked the rest of the way. It was my desire to just appear at the store, which sold groceries and had a small self-service meat market. The radio was on as usual when I arrived, so I didn't pay too much attention to what was on. However, after I had been at work for some time, the announcer suddenly interrupted the regular program to say the president had been shot. That certainly got my attention! Unwelcome scenes began flashing through my mind, striking an unpleasant chord.

I told the boss I had a headache and was going home. He said, "Just because the president's been shot isn't a good enough reason to go home, and I don't want you to go." But I was in no condition to remain at work, so I went home anyway, and it took me a good hour or so to get there. On the way…instead of focusing my attention on Lee and the conspiracy, I was concerned with passersby crying in the streets, and I tried to imagine how people were taking the news in Savannah. Later, I heard there were some who had danced in the streets in celebration of Kennedy's death.

When I got home I turned on the radio to get an update, and learned that the accused assassin had been identified as Lee Harvey Oswald! The announcement indicated that it was an established fact, and I guess I believed what the radio said just because it was the official voice saying so.

I am certain I was in shock all weekend. I felt numb. I knew the president had been killed, and that they were holding Lee responsible, but the full impact of everything was yet to come. I just laid around, hardly eating or sleeping. In fact, I stayed indoors listening to the radio, and like I said…I guess I believed it. This was a major catastrophe in my life. I was a friend of the party who was accused of assassinating the president of the United States. Assassination is a nasty word in any language, and there is no way to justify the evil acts that are committed in the name of liberty. "It's obvious that tyranny rules this system from city hall clear to the presidency!" I thought. According to one definition in the dictionary, assassinations take place because of fanaticism or for a price, but God only knows why it happened in this case. It is no wonder that after three decades of investigation, no satisfactory solution to the case has yet been found. However, after hearing the news of Lee's involvement and learning that everyone seemed so sure that he was the assassin, I began to reassess my own circumstances.

In a movie I once saw on the assassination of President Lincoln, I seemed to recall that people were executed simply because they knew the assassin. It had a tremendous impact on me, and I didn't know how the officials might react to people who knew Lee. I had witnessed three condemned men being taken to their executions, and had gone through the actual experience of sitting in the gas chamber. The whole thing gave me an eerie feeling in my spine as I stayed around the house that weekend, contemplating my future. I didn't have any rules to go by, and I was afraid that perhaps I could be deemed guilty by association. If I hadn't already been in shock because of learning that Lee was being accused of Kennedy's murder, the report the following Sunday that Ruby had killed Lee Harvey Oswald, definitely insured major shock.

Grabbing the paper with Lee's address on it, I struck a match to it. I wouldn't be going to Dallas after all! Knowing I had to leave New Orleans, but not wanting to arouse suspicion, I decided to go to work Monday morning as usual just to play it safe. I was in such a state that my feelings for Lee seemed to have died with him, and it was quite some time before I could begin to react emotionally. I cannot say to this day how long the shock lasted. Could it be that it continued for a quarter of a century? It took me that long to start dealing with the issue by writing this book.

THE GRIM CHOICE

CHAPTER XIII

I knew Ruby, and I knew he was a confederate of Lee's, even if their ideologies were at odds. Lee had compromised his principles in order to be a part of the conspiracy. The way he looked at it, it was an intriguing, clandestine, 007 operation.

But something had gone awry and Lee's plans to warn President Kennedy had backfired. He had been drawn into the plot to kill the president, much like river undercurrents suck those near it into its belly. Now I can look back on everything with hindsight, but I wasn't sure of anything at the time. Even though I knew of the assassination in advance, I was still in a state of shock, traumatized by the events that had taken place. The only thing I knew was that Lee and the president were both dead, and that Lee had been shot by Ruby. Knowing there were people on the inside of the Banister apparatus firing weapons at each other, I was petrified! I existed in a state of uneasiness, afraid they might find out just how much I knew about the conspiracy, and decide to blow me away! Lee was dead and there was no one I could turn to, so I was in a quandry…not knowing what to do.

I realized almost immediately after the assassination that Lee was a patsy as he had claimed, even though I knew he was in on the original plan. It began to dawn on me that the Banister plan had actually gone through. Lee was set up as a patsy, and his death was part of the plan. Ruby had a choice in his own destiny. He could be implicated by Lee, or he could eliminate Lee and be remembered as the man who killed the one person believed to have killed the president. Indeed, he had a grim choice to make, because he would lose either way, no matter how much soul-searching he did between Friday and Sunday. Ruby would rather have been convicted for shooting the accused assassin than for being a part of the conspiracy, and he would have been convicted for sure if Lee had survived.

Monday morning when I went to work, my boss acted suspicious, or maybe it just seemed that way to me. I didn't know but what my involvement with Lee was a criminal offense.

That evening I bought a newspaper and read an article about two young men being arrested and held for federal authorities. Their names were Patrick Martens and Roland Beauboeuf. I was about to dismiss the account when I noticed the address one of them had given…David's Parkway Apartment at 3330 Louisiana! I even got out the paper towel David had written his address on and compared it with the address in the paper…just to make certain; and sure enough, it was the same. It all added up, and I knew then that the Banister assassination plan had gone through. Wondering why David hadn't been picked up, I wasted no time in walking to the gas stove and igniting the paper towel with his address on it. I wondered if there was a candle burning in his apartment or if his mice were starving. "One day he's gonna burn that place down," I thought.

After a sleepless night I forced myself to get dressed and go to work as usual. A policeman in uniform came in and the boss told me he was planning to buy the store, so he asked if I would show him around. That made me nervous. At any other time his reason for being there might not have sounded fishy, but it did then. After I reluctantly took him on a tour of the meat department, he said, "I'll be back tomorrow." I determined right then and there that I wouldn't be there when he came, because he seemed more interested in me than in what I showed him.

My boss apparently had heard me talking about Lee and the election. I must have mentioned Lee's name, because the other store employees distanced themselves from me, and I had a strong feeling I was under suspicion! I felt convinced that the FBI would be the next to visit! Little did I know they weren't interested in anything connected to a conspiracy.

At home that night I read of David's arrest, which made me uneasy because I was afraid I might be implicated. Martens, Beauboeuf and David had been arrested, as ordered by the Secret Service. Furthermore, David was being held on a fugitive warrant from Texas. "Just as I figured," I thought.

"More of those mice die from starvation than from cancer."

David was released on November 27, but I didn't know about it when I left that day at noon because I hadn't read Wednesday's paper; so upon my leaving, I thought he was still in custody. Since he knew me, I was worried that he might not keep his mouth shut, so I breathed a sigh of relief when I knew for sure he hadn't talked.

I had hopes that knowledge of my association and connection to Camp Street might have died with Lee. Not wanting to leave anything to chance, I decided to leave town. I started to burn Lee's picture that had been cut in half, but just couldn't bring myself to do it. After all, he could have killed me that morning in the garage, but he didn't. So I just threw it in the trash instead. By noon the next day I was on the bus heading for Harlengen, Texas. I didn't attempt to collect the two days' pay I had coming, because I was afraid of being arrested if it became known that I was leaving town. The day I left I stopped to get a shoeshine in the bus depot and unknowingly dropped my billfold, containing two-hundred dollars. I didn't realize it until after I left the place, but as soon as I discovered the loss, I immediately went back. I was elated to see the shine boy standing there with my wallet in his hand. I thanked him for returning it, then left. It was my ticket out of town. I have often wondered what I would have done if I hadn't recovered it.

It would be years before I would begin to try to piece together what had happened. I was aware that Ruby and Lee knew each other, yet the media gave the impression that they were complete strangers. As for me, I just wanted to forget the whole affair. It literally made me sick! Before I knew it night had come and I laid my crystal radio down and headed for the bathroom. Seated on the very back seat was a Black girl, probably twenty. "Man, these colored girls are all body," I thought, "and it's this Southern segregation that keeps me from sitting with her." She smiled as I went past.

"Lee was right," I thought, flushing the toilet. "Segregation's a bad thing." Stepping out into the darkness I noticed the girl had scooted over, the lights from a passing car shining on her bare legs. It was an invitation. "Any other time," I thought, anxious to get back to my transistor radio to listen for any updates on the assassination. At least, I knew old Larson was still alive in more ways than one.

I had previously been on the run from the law for writing bad checks, and now I was running again because of the assassination. I had known Banister, Ruby and Shaw, among others, but I didn't know where the chain-of-command ended. Was it the CIA or the FBI? Was it Marcello? I had no way of knowing who to hide from, so I lived under the name, Kenneth Mason in Del Rio, Texas for ten years or so before attempting to return home to Oregon.

I spent many sleepless nights during 1963 and 1964. I was always looking over my shoulder, wondering where the perpetrators might be, curious to know if they were aware that Lee had revealed many secrets of their clandestine operations to me. I always slept with one eye open, a loaded revolver at my side, prepared to protect myself at a moment's notice if they ever discovered my whereabouts and came for me. It was a very stressful time, filled with apprehension and insecurity, never knowing what was around the next corner. To this day I am petrified to stand in front of an uncovered window, afraid of being fired at. At times the feelings are so intense that I can almost feel the bullet.

I managed to get a job at a ranch in Santa Maria near Harlengen. My boss, Mr. Dunn, had a cannery in LaFaria, a nearby town. One of my jobs was to build a slaughter house on the ranch where people would come to buy meat, and the other job was helping tend to a herd of beef cattle. I tried to distance myself from what had happened in New Orleans, but during those long fall nights alone in the ranch house, I found myself entering those events in my diary. I was at Santa Maria five months before I realized that if anyone ever read what I had written, I could be questioned and forced to go before government committees, which I wasn't prepared to do. I didn't know it at the time, but I wouldn't be ready for over twenty-five years.

Lee didn't have anything personal against the president, and felt there were no prior incidents that would connect him to the killing. The shooting of Connally, though, was a different matter. Lee hadn't fired a shot, and he knew he had wiped his fingerprints from the rifle the last time he'd used it, as he always did. This took place prior to September 23. Marina claimed she saw Lee cleaning his rifle several times, and yet no cleaning materials were ever found. I suspect he was actually cleaning fingerprints from his rifle, rather than cleaning the barrel or the firing chamber.

After the assassination there wasn't enough time for Lee to have removed fingerprints from the weapon, as only ninety seconds elapsed from the time the president was shot to the moment he was encountered at the Coke machine on the second floor of the book depository. In fact, Lee may not have known his rifle had even been removed from his place of residence, since he had denied taking it with him to work.

Chemical tests on both Lee's cheeks proved negative, showing that he had not fired a rifle that day. Again, when confronted by a police officer at the pop machine on the second floor of the depository, he seemed calm. It is my belief, based on conversations with Lee, that he wasn't on the run until he found out the assassin had shot Connally.

In November 1988, on the 25th anniversary of the assassination, a book came out entitled *The Great Expectations of John Connally*. It was eventually published under the title of *Lone Star, The Life of John Connally*, written by James Reston and given a cover story by *Time* magazine. It was captioned *Was Connally the Real Target?* This particular edition of Time received wide coverage and attention. Because of the testimony I have described, it is inconceivable to me that he was the target. At the time of the assassination it was firmly established that because of the strings that attached him to Connally, Lee was his protector. He knew that if anything happened to the governor he would be considered a suspect, something we had discussed very thoroughly. Lee panicked when he realized Connally was hit, and this is what put him on the run. I clearly remember what Lee said, "When you kill for vengeance, dig two graves." This is my opinion as to what happened, and how I think Lee would have reacted because of being connected to the Connally shooting:

Lee was on the first floor of the Texas School Book Depository at the time of the shooting. He had gotten change from the office and gone upstairs to the second floor. An officer saw him drinking a coke at the pop machine on the second floor of the book depository just ninety seconds after the shooting. When the officer drew his gun, Lee's supervisor said, "He's okay; he works here." Lee's rifle was allegedly found on the sixth floor, where three bullet casings had been carefully placed. The rifle had no fingerprints on it, but later a palm print appeared on the stock, probably from Lee's dead hand.

It is my conjecture that when White, in the vicinity of the book depository, came in contact with Tippit in his patrol car, he got in and directed: "Take me to 1026 Beckley; we need to pick up someone and take him to Red Bird."

Lee took a taxi home to the address on Beckley. As he went in the landlady said, "The president's been shot!" Lee hurried past, saying nothing. She said, "Oh, I see you're in a hurry." He rushed to his room, changed into another shirt and grabbed a coat and his pistol from its hiding place in the air conditioner. Meanwhile, the landlady saw a patrol car with two policemen in it pull up in front. They honked twice, then drove off. Lee left abruptly, without saying a word. He walked outside, turned left on Beckley, and walked about half a block to where the patrol car was waiting.

He got inside with the two uniformed men, officers Roscoe White and J.D. Tippit. White began filling Lee in on the assassination. "Somebody screwed up and shot Connally," he said. Lee was furious! He knew he would be considered a suspect because of the letter he had written regarding his discharge. Lee and White began arguing. Lee yelled at White, "When Connally got shot, I got set up!" When it became obvious to Tippit that they had been in on the president's death, he exclaimed, "Hey! You guys need the old seventy-two!" He slammed on the brakes abruptly, skidding to a halt on the corner of 10th and Patton, probably to handcuff them.

In the commotion Lee escaped on foot. Tippit jumped out of the car and White shot him, then fled from the scene. Three bullets were later removed from Tippit's body; two 38 Special Winchester Westerns, and one Remington Peters. Four shots were fired in all, and four cartridge casings were found at the scene. They all contained the markings that an automatic weapon makes when fired. Lee's gun was not an automatic. When he was apprehended in the Texas Theatre he had a fully-loaded 38 Special revolver with a 2 ¼ inch barrel, which contained six unfired bullets in the cylinder, and he had no extra bullets in his possession. It was never tested to see if it had been recently fired. It would have been absurd for him to take the time to eject cartridges from his revolver at the scene of the killing, which would have been necessary from a non-automatic gun where spent cartridges are held in the cylinder. Obviously, Lee had not shot Tippit.

I made a clean break from the assassination except for what remained in Banister's files. Evidently the government that may yet have those files in its possession, doesn't want them made available to the public for obvious reasons. Since the release of Oliver Stone's movie, "JFK," there has been a renewed interest in having all files released, but I can assure you the Banister files will never see the light of day, because they would indicate a conspiracy!

For twenty-five years following Kennedy's murder, I watched government committees work on the case, and I read about Shaw's conspiracy trial and his subsequent acquittal, but I still did not come forward. From 1972 onward, I never did hide the fact that I had known Lee. After I returned home that year, my family asked me not to get involved in anything concerning the assassination, which seemed easy enough to do at the time.

You might wonder why I'm coming forward now after such a long time of silence. Well, I can't answer that any more than I can answer why I never came forth for any hearings or subsequent trials, such as in the case of the Shaw trial in New Orleans. I think the answer may lie within the Oregon prison system. I was incarcerated there into an adult prison at an early age, a place where one could easily be dehumanized into a state of near-vegetation. It has taken many years for me to undo to any extent what the state of Oregon taught me in prison. It should not be surprising that I was involved in prison reform movements for a period of time after returning to Oregon in 1972.

In prison we were taught to play our cards close to the chest, to do our own time and not worry about others. It should come as no great surprise that I kept silent about my conversations with Lee and my knowledge of the president's impending assassination. Perhaps if the state of Oregon had better rehabilitation programs instead of simply warehousing humans, Jack Kennedy would be in Florida right now, basking in the sun with Jackie, enjoying the golden years. I knew about the plans to murder Kennedy, and did nothing to prevent it. That has been a heavy burden to carry around on my shoulders all these years.

Because of my personal involvement in the conspiracy and because of what I know about Ruby, I feel it's critical to expose his true intentions. I want the world to know the actual motive behind Ruby's actions when he shot Lee Harvey Oswald. The story must not end with the view that the all-American Jack Ruby gunned down the deranged assassin of his beloved President in an act of patriotism! That is simply not the way it was!

IN LEE'S DEFENSE

CHAPTER XIV

It would be impossible to vindicate Lee from being connected to the assassination. He was in on it and I am a witness to that. However, the apparent degree of his guilt can be lessened considerably by those such as myself who are able, in a sense, to speak from the grave for Lee.

The day Kennedy was killed, I didn't intend to leave New Orleans and run out on Lee, leaving him in the lurch. I felt certain I would testify in his behalf, and the CIA faction I was associated with would get their share of blame for the killing. I was sure Lee would be vindicated, and even if complete vindication wasn't possible, surely his seeming degree of guilt upon due process of law would have been much lighter than history has attributed to him.

When Lee was killed, it changed the course of my life. He had intended for me to be his witness when he pointed the finger at the true assassins, but how high above the Banister apparatus their connections were, I have no way of knowing. He now had to deal with the paper trail that tied him to Connally, and this was a problem of an even higher magnitude than the concern over Kennedy.

My importance to Lee is shown by his return to New Orleans on October 11, to make sure that I hadn't divulged any of the things he had confided to me. I lived under the same fears and expectations that he had experienced as we saw the assassination developing together. He had done one significant thing to connect me to him. He had me fill out the change-of-address card for him and deposit it in the LaFayette branch of the post office. Lee didn't dream, of course, that a postal employee would fill out a new one because I had printed his name where the signature was required.

In 1990 when I was in Dallas, an assassination researcher, Gary Shaw, located a copy of the card. The writing on it was neither mine nor Lee's. I printed his name on the one I turned in, because I didn't want my handwriting on it, and Lee had told me, "Well, then print it. It's okay if you print it." So that's what I did, although I worried about it for more than two decades. I was concerned about a possible connection to the plot being proven through my printing on the card. As it turned out, the original card had obviously been disposed of.

I considered coming forward to expose the conspiracy, after the assassination…before Lee was shot. I thought of going to the news media rather than the authorities, but before I could act, Lee was killed. After his death I saw no reason to expose myself, since it was too late to help him; and because of what Ruby had done, everything seemed crazy and mixed-up. I was frightened of Banister and the authorities, afraid of the Cubans and a man named Carlos.

After leaving New Orleans in 1963 and spending some time on a ranch at Santa Maria near Harlengen, I went to McAllen, Texas, where I worked for Beno's Quality Meats. There I met an eighteen-year-old named Nathan Bales. When I left McAllen, he went with me to Arkansas, where we spent a couple of weeks, then we stayed a short time in New Orleans, where I went by the name of Robert C. Larson, while employed by Meydrich's Fine Meats, Inc. Later I left Nathan in New Orleans and eventually ended up in Del Rio, Texas, where I remained until 1972. I lived there under the name of Kenneth Mason.

On December 8, 1992, Lessie Young Coloma located Nathan's telephone number after a brief investigation, and called him at his home in Sedona, Arizona.

"Do you remember Ron Larson from 1964?" she asked.

"Yes, I remember him," he responded, "but I always had the feeling that Larson wasn't his real name."

"You were right," she replied. "His name is really Ron Lewis."

They talked at length about various things that related to the time Nathan and I were close friends. He told her that I had been very sick and was using the Christian Science textbook, which teaches mind-over-matter, as a cure. Incidentally, the sickness I had was an ulcer, which did not respond to the treatment. Nathan told my collaborator, "Ron Larson really had a big influence on my life." After their conversation ended, Lessie told me, "There's certainly no doubt in my mind that Ron Larson and Ron Lewis are one and the same."

After I arrived in Del Rio I went to work for Rain's Produce. My boss's name was Carlos Rains, and when I heard his given name, it rang a bell deep inside me. It reminded me of another Carlos, who represented events of a violent and clandestine nature. Disturbing thoughts of the assassination flashed through my mind! I asked myself, "Couldn't my involvement in it have been only a nightmare? Did it necessarily have to be real?"

Only a short time had passed since the tragic events, and the memories were still very vivid. I had tried to distance myself, but every time I heard the name "Carlos," it brought back memories of Lee. He always had a note of irritation in his voice when he mentioned that name.

While writing this book I have tried to remember all I could about this man, because he was involved in the assassination, and everyone at 544 Camp Street moved aside to let him pass. I wanted to remember all I could about him, and because I had tried to block certain incidents out of my mind, I became interested in psychological memory techniques.

In the October 1989 issue of the *Journal of Applied Psychology*, there was information presented on memory techniques that the police were using to help solve crimes. It was still in the laboratory stages. The publication stated that by analyzing interviews with robbery victims and witnesses, they found that seven detectives trained in the technique elicited forty-seven per cent more results than did nine untrained detectives. I was interested in being able to remember things I had blocked out because of the terrible shock of the assassination.

Consequently, I wrote to R. Edward Geiselman of the University of California, informing him of my concern and my reason for wanting to be questioned by that method. I never received a response.

After I began writing this book, I contracted a typist and a collaborator. They helped me immensely with my memory problems. Also, revisiting the sites where the conspiracy took place has been helpful. Speaking in Lee's defense is not an easy task, because he wanted to be an assassin. In the reader's eyes, this might portray him as President Kennedy's assassin, and I don't want to create that impression.

The chemical tests made of Lee's cheeks on the day of the murder were negative. This should give credibility to the statements that he never fired a rifle. If due process of law had been provided for him, this would have weighed heavily in his defense. As far as Lee was concerned, great leaders have humble beginnings, and he saw himself as just that. However, he realized that he possessed fatal obsessions, and his impulse to eliminate his political opposition was uncontrollable.

Once I met a boy who seemed to have a unique way of solving almost any problem that confronted him. He would blast it with a double-barreled laser beam and smash it to pieces. Of course the object in reality was still there, but to him it had disappeared. Lee had these same impulses except for one difference. At times these figments of the mental realm would surface into the real world.

While in Moscow Lee wrote his brother a letter that peers into his world, not unlike any great political hopeful in exile. He was a product of this system, one made up of varying man-made governments, of which the Bible states, "It does not belong to man who is walking even to direct his steps."

(Jeremiah 10:23) In fact, in a publication called *Examining the Scriptures Daily,* it states something to that effect, and would apply in this case. "Humans are endowed with truly remarkable mental capacity, but they were not made with the ability to steer a successful course through life without humbly accepting help from God." (12)

In his letter to his brother, Lee states: "Because the government supports an economic system based on credit, which gives rise to the never-ending cycle of depression, inflation, unlimited speculation, which is the phase America is in now, and war...Look around you and look at yourself. See the segregation, the unemployment and what automation is." (13)

When Lee and I talked about these concerns, his kidding manner disappeared and he was dead serious, as these were legitimate concerns. The system which confronted him and alienated him, just did not work. What's more, it never would as far as he was concerned, and this is what Lee revolted against. Perhaps if he hadn't been fatally obsessed and attracted to subversiveness, he might have aspired to political office. "After all," Lee said, "Harry Truman didn't have a college education." It worried him a great deal though, that he didn't have complete control over himself. He was plagued with fatal obsessions and greatly depended on his mentor for continued survival in the realm of the real world. Perhaps this is why he supported gun control. (14)

Matters were made worse when Lee fell into the hands of the conspirators. Even though he displayed a great deal of resistance, the aspect became irresistible to him in its conclusion. When he left New Orleans on September 25, he would be without a mentor from then on.

I suppose there were many Lees in the land. Certainly there

were things in the present system that young men would find objectionable. But this particular Lee had the traits of an assassin and would be a prime candidate for a patsy. What they hadn't counted on was that I would be there to see it take place, and would eventually record it for the human record. I was aware of nearly every move and motive of the ongoing scheme to murder the president, except for the actual method of carrying it out. And I even had a hint of that, because Lee told me about Roscoe White and how he had been selected to shoot the president, although I did not know at the time that the plan was in its infancy.

Today, conspiracy publications and claims are greeted with skepticism. One such claim in Lee's defense appeared in the newspapers on August 7, 1990, and was given a good deal of national attention and wide coverage. Ricky White claimed his father, Roscoe White, killed Kennedy on CIA orders. The FBI and CIA said such claims were ludicrous and not credible. They flatly denied that the CIA was involved in any way in the assassination. The Warren Commission concluded that Oswald acted alone. Ricky's statement corroborates the conclusion made by a divided house committee in 1978 that there was more than one gunman. His mother, Geneva Galle, told the *Odessa American* newspaper there was no doubt in her mind that her husband killed Kennedy. White, who lives in Midland Texas, said his father joined the Dallas Police Department in 1963 to prepare for carrying out the assassination. He said that Oswald was part of the conspiracy, but that he fired no shots. He also stated that his father killed officer J.D. Tippit. White believes a CIA elimination squad killed his father in 1971.

At first, even though I had learned about Roscoe White

from Lee in 1963, I didn't want to appear overwhelmed by the White account, because I had suffered enough on the issue of skepticism. It plagues me to this day, but even so I am dedicated to relating truthful information, and I am not going to doctor up this account for the benefit of skeptics.

Mrs. White died of a heart attack in February 1991. Before her death I tried to contact her through the *Odessa American.* But considering the luck I always seem to have with the media, I received no response.

An article in the December 1990 issue of the *Texas Monthly* magazine, related an account of Geneva attempting to reproduce her husband's diary, because the FBI had stolen the original. It appears that she produced the fake document because of pressure put on her to come up with something new and persuasive. Mrs. White received $5,300 for the diary, part of which was paid by Oliver Stone. This didn't help her cause any, because it gave the whole thing a ring of fraud. You might say that her method of defending her story torpedoed the White account, although some Dallas researchers give it credibility. I can testify to the fact that Lee told me White was to be Kennedy's assassin, but I cannot confirm who actually pulled the trigger.

During the production of the "JFK" movie in Dallas in 1991, I interviewed a man named Ed Hoffman, who actually witnessed the assassination. He would have been a key witness had he been given the opportunity to testify. Hoffman is a deaf mute. He said he tried to tell a policeman on the scene what he saw, and with all the excitement of looking for the assassins, the police shoved him aside. Because of that incident, Hoffman was reluctant to come forward for many years. Later when he decided to talk, he was interviewed on a British tele-

212

PHOTO I TOOK OF ED HOFFMAN IN DALLAS IN 1991.

vision talk show, which was not aired in the United States. Upon hearing about the movie, he decided to tell what he knew about the incident.

When I first met the Hoffmans, I saw a beautiful girl using her hands to talk to her parents, and I thought she was a deaf mute. When she began talking, I was surprised to learn that it was Hoffman and not his daughter who was mute. We toured the assassination site and he gave his account of what happened, partly by using sign language and partly by writing notes. Mr. Hoffman said he had been on the freeway at the time of Kennedy's murder, and had a good view of the grounds behind the picket fence. He wrote a note which said,

*THIS IS THE PICKET FENCE OFTEN ALLUDED TO IN CONNEC-
TION WITH THE ASSASSINATION.*

"I saw two men behind the fence. One man wearing a black hat and blue jacket fired a rifle at the motorcade, and then gave it to the other man and walked away." Could it have been Roscoe White? Hoffman continued, "The second man disassembled the rifle and put it in a toolbox and walked toward the railroad."

The writers of this book made an investigation of the Jack Lawrence involvement, which motivates the question…was the second man Jack Lawrence? The government and Mr. Lawrence have one thing in common. Their involvements were on the same periphery; denials and coverups in spite of overwhelming evidence to the contrary.

Mr. Hoffman told me the FBI tried to pay him to say nothing of what he had seen. According to what Lee told me about White being the man who was to kill Kennedy, along with Hoffman's testimony, I ask the question: "Do you think one of the two men behind the picket fence was Roscoe White?"

And what about Jack Lawrence? His car was found behind the fence.

The White account seems to have left a bad taste in everyone's mouth. Apparently, because of Geneva's deceitfulness in reproducing the diary, it has been omitted from Oliver Stone's movie on the assassination, although Oliver has video tapes of my testimony on White. The scene involving the picket fence was in the movie, but the gunman behind the fence had no name. No matter what might be the outcome, I will not compromise, and have never concealed my knowledge of White's involvement in the assassination. The credibility of the White account is at stake. Was Roscoe White the man behind the picket fence?

Mrs. White had connections to the Banister apparatus, besides what was brought out in the article in the media. Geneva White Galle had worked as a stripper for Jack Ruby at his Carousel Club in Dallas and Jack worked for Banister and considered himself a CIA contract agent, like David Ferrie. In 1976 the Senate Intelligence Committee found a pose of Lee in a series of pictures in the possession of a Dallas policeman's widow, the former Mrs. Roscoe White. She informed the committee that her husband had told her to hang onto the photo, because someday it would be worth a lot of money.

In 1976 Mrs. White's husband had been dead five years, and she knew he had left a diary confessing his part in the murder. No matter how deeply I might have been involved in the assassination, I didn't want it to be made public for a long time, and I am sure this is the way Mrs. White felt. There was nothing she could do to change the situation, so she remained silent until she felt safe in coming forward, as I have done.

What impresses me is that my factual account supports the

White story, because it has been stated that Roscoe was acting on CIA orders when he shot the president. In my account, I revealed the fact that I knew of a plot to kill the president. It involved the CIA faction that I worked for, which included Lee Oswald and Roscoe White. Roscoe was hired on October 7, 1963 by the Dallas Police Department at the time the conspiracy was developing before me at 544 Camp Street. The fact that Lee told me White was in his Marine unit and that Ruby was the Dallas contact, was impressive. I later found out about Ruby's close ties to the Dallas Police Department.

It's no wonder that all I received from the FBI was what amounted to a "thank-you" note, when I gave them my account through Congressman Defazio of Oregon. It reads: "Congressman Peter Defazio has forwarded your account of your relationship with Lee Harvey Oswald and information relating to the assassination of President John F. Kennedy to the FBI. It was thoughtful of you to make this material available. It has been referred to our investigative division for information and review." It was signed John E. Collingwood.

At least the testimony I gave to Congressman Defazio wasn't termed as "ludicrous" and "not credible"...just that they were going to investigate it, and it probably got filed away somewhere to hopefully be forgotten. An element of the CIA did plan and carry out the assassination. Every time this is brought to light, the CIA and FBI deny it and use words such as "ludicrous" and "not credible," in order to make the informant appear ridiculous.

I know the FBI was deeply involved, because the Banister apparatus planned the assassination. When Mr. Banister died a year later the FBI cleaned out his office, leaving behind only what they thought would be non-incriminating. This account was described in Jim Garrison's book, *Heritage of Stone.*

If Banister had no active role in the FBI as he had in the past, why would they be interested in leaving his office bare? This is odd, because when the government investigation of the president's murder was in progress, they could find nothing that interested them at 544 Camp Street. However, a study of secret service report CO-2-34-030 shows that my testimony is vital to any subsequent investigations, because the report said it was impossible to find anyone who recalls ever seeing Lee Harvey Oswald at that address. Not only did I see Lee at 544 Camp Street many times, but it is all on record in the files that the FBI confiscated in 1964.

When investigating a murder, any armchair detective can tell you that the person with the strongest motive is considered the guilty party, so let us do some probing. We will begin with the accused, Lee Harvey Oswald. What motive would he have to assassinate Kennedy? A study by the author revealed that a posthumous evaluation of Oswald was made by a psychiatrist working for the government, who called attention to Lee's unusually poor spelling. It was concluded that the frustrating effect of his spelling disability would not be inconsistent with his decision to murder the president. What a farce! This is typical of government attempts to come up with motives to ascribe to Lee Oswald, and it is certainly humorous, to say the least!

Speaking as Lee's best friend, I have not heard one single motive that would have been a sufficient basis for him to fire the shot that killed Kennedy, even though he was involved to some extent. The only indication I had of his participation, was that he no longer made any moves to get out of the assassination plot from September 15 onward.

Secondly, we will consider the racial segregationist elements. I realize that a book could be written on this subject, so I will be brief and just deal with motives. As I have stated, I lived in Savannah while Kennedy was in his mid-term. The majority who were vocal were breathing death threats against the president because of his stand on integration. In fact, J. Edgar Hoover, was also against integration. This was a serious threat to the president, and we were made aware of this by the assassination of Medgar Evers, the NAACP field leader that was gunned down in Jackson, Mississippi. I won't go into this anymore than necessary in order to show a motive for killing the president.

Next, we will consider the anti-Castro network that Kennedy betrayed when he informed them in a speech that the Cuban flag would fly again in Havana. The Bay of Pigs survivors had brought it back with them when they were released from captivity. When I was in New Orleans in 1963, the Banister apparatus was servicing this element. It was the vehicle that planned out the assassination and also had the support of the anti-Castros. I am not attempting to show who had a motive to plan out the assassination, as I already know the answer. But I am trying to show who might have had a reason to employ them.

Next we will consider the Mafia. Kennedy had accepted their assistance in getting elected, but later turned against them. As a senator, he had stepped on the toes of the Mafia. And as president, by refusing to topple the Castro government, he had denied the Mafia their Havana gambling casinos. One who should be considered as a prime suspect in the plot to kill the president was Carlos Marcello, Louisiana crime boss and Banister associate. As I alluded to earlier, the

Kennedys kidnapped Marcello and flew him to Argentina, leaving him in a desolate and lonely place where he almost died. Did he have reason to kill Kennedy? Yes, without doubt, he had a motive and he certainly had made that threat.

The next element to consider is something most Americans seem reluctant to come to grips with. Did the United States government have anything to do with the assassination of President Kennedy? As I have said, a government agency planned the assassination, namely the Banister apparatus. It's connection to the government comes to the fore when one considers that the FBI confiscated Banister's files when he died in 1964.

John F. Kennedy's increasing popularity and his pursuit for peace, meant people like Banister and his apparatus would soon lose their status. Kennedy's death was secretly approved of by many powerful men the government had produced. This silent approval should be interpreted as a massive government conspiracy against Kennedy. Yes, it was one thing to speak of peace but another to actually withdraw troops from Vietnam, where a battle was raging. The CIA was deeply entrenched in it and had no desire to give it up.

When President Kennedy opened the way for peace talks with Castro, powerful government men muttered behind closed doors. This was done against the advice of his chiefs-of-staff when he signed the nuclear test ban treaty in Moscow. The CIA invaded Cuba, and the president withheld air support. Kennedy's survival would mean a loss of power for these powerful men, along with CIA agents like Banister. That is why they gave silent consent to his assassination. After taking office Johnson rescinded Kennedy's de-escalation plans and increased the number of troops in Vietnam. Apparently

Kennedy's death had been in the interests of many, and had the silent approval of those dissenting Kennedy policies.

Those rallying to the cause of a free democratic Cuba joined forces with Banister. They also enjoyed local diplomatic immunity. All this contributed to his success, which included a nod from the FBI. They were believed to be CIA in their region, even though they actually evolved. They were not outwardly acknowledged by the government as appointed individuals, but were to give the impression that they assumed their positions like many in the CIA. It was this type of Cyclopean agency that President Kennedy had ordered to be put out of business. Those elements were disobeying orders, such as continuing the assassination attempts on Castro, and arming the Cuban anti-Castro community. Finally, he had a controversy with the segment that accused him of leaving missiles in Cuba after the decoys were removed. Banister, in a rage, was kicking things and sailing them around in his office. He yelled, "That bastard, Kennedy let the Russians take out the decoys and leave the real McCoys!" Banister was truly a thorn in the president's side...or was it vice versa?

With the anti-Castro element expelled from their homeland and exiled in the United States, a state of war existed. They came here seeking asylum, planning to regroup and retake their homeland. Democracy was appealing to them, and it seemed that the United States would be supportive of that all the way. However, political maneuvering on a global scale left the refugees hanging in the wind, victims of a broken promise. Under such conditions anyone who opposed their movement, even President Kennedy, would naturally become their bitter enemy. In fact, because he at first supported the anti-Castro effort and then did a reversal, Kennedy became a traitor to the cause. Unless we had been actively involved, we could not be expected to comprehend the magnitude of the bitterness that existed within the anti-Castro community.

Additionally, the particular CIA factions, such as Banister's, came into a life-and-death struggle with the Kennedy brothers for their continued existence. By his actions, Kennedy had assured himself of an assassination. The reasons for the decision to do away with him had been established; the only thing lacking was an element to carry out the act. His political empire was too powerful for him to be impeached. His popularity with the people was at its highest peak, so there was no other alternative ...assassination was the only answer! The Banister apparatus, complete with Lee Harvey Oswald as patsy, was ripe for the job. With so many factions out to get Kennedy, including those within the government, there was no escape for him. If it did not take place in Dallas, it would happen elsewhere.

I am sure these things crossed Lee's mind at one point, and had something to do with his decision to join the Banister plan. There were literally millions of dollars available for the operation, and they had the means for accomplishing their goal. What they could not get done for money, they could have done by appealing to one's sense of patriotism, since Kennedy was a national security threat.

Some have said that the slacking off of Kennedy's security by the Secret Service would net an assassination. A government-connected right-wing element carried it out with the nod of powerful men, such as J. Edgar Hoover and men within the CIA, even the chiefs-of-staff. Lyndon Johnson could not have been ignorant of that fact, and I've always thought a book should be written, entitled *The Two Faces of*

Lyndon Johnson. The antics of President Kennedy could no longer be ignored. These men now considered him a threat to the security of the United States, as well as to their continued employment in their respective agencies.

I suspect the bottom line, the chief reason why Kennedy was executed had to do with money, his signing Executive Order 11 and 110, which called for the issuing of $4,292,893,815 in U.S. notes through the traditional Reserve System. Kennedy apparently reasoned that by returning to the Constitution, which states that only Congress shall coin and regulate money, the soaring national debt could be reduced drastically by not having to pay interest to the bankers of the Federal Reserve System who print paper money then loan it to the government at high interest rates.

According to information from the Library of the Comptroller of the Currency, the same executive order that Kennedy signed in 1963 remains in effect today. This is the case, although successive administrations beginning with that of President Lyndon Johnson apparently have simply ignored it and returned to the practice of paying interest on Federal Reserve notes.

These notes continue to be used today and the national deficit is at an all-time peak. Although Kennedy's efforts to reform the money supply were not too widely-noted, some assassination researchers believe this may have cost him a great deal more than just the enmity of the powerful international bankers of the Federal Reserve System.

Bo Gritz, a 1992 candidate for the presidency, who was the most decorated Green Beret commander, Intelligence officer and Reconnaissance chief, recognized the role that the Federal Reserve System played in the current economic crisis. During his campaign he stated, "It makes no sense to pay usury on our own money, and Federal Reserve banks use the national debt as collateral. Through "fractionalized banking," they lend many times that amount of interest back to the people."

One interesting statement Mr. Gritz made was that the FED has never been audited since assuming the Congressional responsibility for legal tender in 1913. We might ask ourselves, "Who stood the most to gain from Kennedy's death?" Was it the powerful "Big Business" tycoons who owned the Federal Reserve System and would realize a tremendous financial loss if the U.S. returned to having currency coined and regulated by Congress instead of by the FED? Or did they merely give silent consent to the assassination, with the end results the same as if they had actually pulled the trigger?

OCTOBER 11, 1963

CHAPTER XV

Lee had read a story in a James Bond novel where the famous spy was supposed to be in his room asleep but was out cutting his capers. The two crooks in the story had no inkling they were being watched, since they thought Bond was in his room. From this story Lee got the idea to return to New Orleans without anyone knowing that he had ever left town. It was a very ingenious plan because for three decades the whole world thought he was in Dallas that day. His clever plan showed that Lee planned his escapades quite well.

After telling his landlady Mrs. Bledsoe on Thursday

evening that he would be in his room all day Friday and not to disturb him, he crawled out of his second-story window and probably went down a tree to the ground, then boarded a bus for New Orleans. It was about a 12-hour ride, and he would have enough time to reach his destination on Friday morning, take care of business and leave New Orleans in enough time to return to Dallas by early Saturday morning.

The record clearly shows that Lee had a friend in New Orleans during the summer of 1963, because someone unidentified at that time filled out and filed a change-of-address card for him at the LaFayette sub-post office. I was the one who filled out that card for him, but was hesitant to put my handwriting on it for obvious reasons, so I printed it. Lee told me I didn't have to sign his name, that the information was sufficient. However, the postal clerk apparently didn't feel the same, because when I examined a copy of the document in 1990 it was in handwriting and was properly signed. It's obvious that the clerk is the one who filled out the new one and signed it.

The writing was neither mine nor Lee's, but I initiated the card, not by a phone call as some suspect, but by turning in a document that needed a change before it was acceptable. A lot has been written about his friend, and some want this individual to stay out there in the shadows somewhere and never surface. However, it is time for me to come forth and make the truth known after more than 25 years of evading detection.

I'm sure there are parts of this book that could be doctored or left out, with the objective of convincing publishers of it's reliability. An example would be the claim that Lee went to Canada on his trip to Mexico or his all-night trip to New Orleans on October 11. Maybe the book would be more attractive to publishers that are interested in it as a monetary object if these items were omitted. But would that be fair to the public, to Lee, or to the only living witness to his activities? A following chapter will deal with the problems the author has encountered in his determination to present this book to the people in its pure form. For this reason, self-publication was chosen by the author.

My last conversation with Lee was on October 11, 1963. While I am hesitant to introduce any new evidence that might confuse researchers and publishers, I still must do so in the interests of truth. The historical record has been deprived of the facts about Lee's visit to New Orleans on the above date. However, I'm making every effort to see that this missing piece of history is inserted into the proper niche of the record, even though it's thirty years overdue!

According to our conversation on that date, there was more to Lee's placement at the Texas School Book Depository than has been brought out by the record. Lee told me on October 11 that Jack Ruby had secured a job for him at the depository.

Regardless of the consensus in the historical records and various publications, we discussed this matter in depth on October 11, because Lee wanted me to go to Dallas after the election, which would be on December 7. He told me he would have an income and a place for me to stay when I got to Dallas. He said he might be in the newspapers, which caused my old fears to resurface. If I were to continue being Lee's friend, I would prefer that he conduct himself in a non-conspicuous manner because of my being a fugitive. I was afraid I would begin to see the same old Lee reappearing.

He talked of moving from Marsalis Street to an apartment the two of us could share. In 1991 I visited the place he told me about and it wouldn't have been big enough. He must have been relying on someone else's description, because I'm sure if he'd seen it, he would have agreed that it was too small.

DEALING WITH THE
ASSASSINATION

CHAPTER XVI

By 1964 I began rewriting my diary, which has been in my brother's safe since 1972. It shows that I had no intentions of being involved in the subsequent investigations I read about in the newspaper. I remember weighing the risks of coming forward, and as always, I declined. Lee had informed me of everything I would need to know in order to testify, but it would've been necessary for him to live before he could activate any such plan. I would have come forward if Lee had lived, but after his death I knew I had to erase all tracks that might associate me with him. I always knew, however, that at some future time I would tell this story.

I have read several books on the assassination-written by several authors. Some have come close to the truth, such as Robert Morrow, whom Lee and I discussed. However, at the time-he was probably going by the name of Robert Porter. I remember him by the incident we discussed...his trip to Cuba with David Ferrie the time David was wounded. In his book *Betrayal*, Morrow stated that Lee had gone to Canada during his trip to Mexico, and I can confirm that.

In order for Morrow to have knowledge of that incident, he had to have had inside information not available to the general authority. In addition, there is something very interesting about his book, as he tells of Lee burying his rifle and pistol at his old Neely Street address in Dallas prior to going to New Orleans. I know for a fact this was a lie that Lee told to Banister, and Morrow picked up on it. Banister had asked, "Where's your rifle, Lee?" And Lee answered, "In Dallas, at my old Neely Street address, wrapped in plastic, buried under some bushes." I saw the rifle in New Orleans around the end of August 1963. Morrow's information stemmed from a lie that Lee told, which very few people knew about outside of the actual conspirators. I wonder how Morrow knew of this lie; very interesting indeed. He also knew about the trip to Canada.

On the October 11 visit, as discussed previously, Lee and I talked about the trip to Canada that he made when he went to Mexico. I do not know the details of how that plan was conceived or for what reason. I just know that it transpired. Lee didn't tell Marina about going on to Canada during the trip to Mexico, which surely must have taken a lot of self-restraint on his part, because he liked to talk of his exploits. What he did not tell Marina is important, because it shows what the content of the meeting in Canada was about. Since the Walker incident, he wouldn't confide in her anymore on the subject of assassinations.

Lee was afraid he could no longer trust Marina with such a confidential matter as the plot to assassinate Kennedy. Besides, she liked Kennedy and Lee well knew it. The Canadian trip was, no doubt, connected to the assassination or he would have discussed it with Marina.

Because of Castro's September alignment with Banister's scheme, Lee was sent on that mission because of his known support for Cuba. At that time Banister didn't know he wasn't dealing with Castro. Lee was the only Banister operative who outwardly had shown such support for Cuba, which was consistent with the Banister method of operation. I seem to remember that the person he met in Canada was Che Guevera or one of his operatives. After that visit, he told me he no longer felt strongly supportive of Che. Evidently, they hadn't seen eye-to-eye on some matter. This meeting took place between September 25 and October 3. Lee returned to Dallas with his ironclad alibi that he had been in Mexico, applied for a Cuban passport and was turned down.

David Ferrie made a phone call September 24 to a Chicago number, Whitehall 4-4970. This confirms, in addition to my testimony, that he had a connection to Ruby. It was the phone number of Jean West, who appeared at the Cabana Motel with a Lawrence Myers in Dallas, where Ruby visited them the day before the assassination. There is more on that meeting in various publications, but I mentioned it in this chapter to substantiate what I have already related that shows Ferrie was connected to Ruby, and Ruby to the Banister operation.

I first learned of Jack Ruby from my friend Nelva Jean in Fort Worth. As I have said, her husband Floyd sometimes worked with Karen Carlin's husband, Bruce. I saw Karen on more than one occasion when she brought Nelva Jean to my apartment. I had occasionally loaned Karen money for bus fare to attend the amateur nights at Jack Ruby's night club. I specifically remember when I first met her. I was nervous because Nelva Jean placed me on a kind of pedestal and it was embarrassing for me. Nelva also knew I was a fugitive and had probably told Karen about it, but such secrets were safe among my friends, so I didn't worry about it. It could have been because I classed them with those on about the second rung of the social ladder.

Perhaps there might have been other things that made such secrets safe with them...I don't know. Anyway, I liked Karen and she was intriguing to me, so I was sorry to hear of her death shortly after Kennedy's assassination. She was murdered at twenty years of age, as I recall. About the time I left Fort Worth to go to Dallas, Karen had been promoted from her job at Jack Kirkwood's Cellar, to working as a stripper for her husband's boss, Jack Ruby, at his night club in Dallas. She had stepped up to a situation that would claim her life.

It is interesting to map Bruce Carlin's movements on the weekend of Kennedy's murder. He was in Houston on November 21, the day of the presidential parade, and left that same day for New Orleans, where he spent Friday. David was in New Orleans the day Bruce was there, and Bruce was an employee of Jack Ruby. On Saturday evening, November 23, Bruce arrived back in Fort Worth, where he and Karen drove to Dallas and made a call to Jack Ruby from a pay phone at a parking lot. They were accompanied by Nancy Powell, Ralph Paul's girlfriend. This shows some close ties between the Carlins and Ralph Paul, Ruby's partner.

When the secret service personnel interviewed Karen on November 24, 1963, this was the content of the record:

"Mrs. Carlin was highly agitated and was reluctant to make any statement to me. She stated to me that she was under the impression that Lee Harvey Oswald, Jack Ruby and other individuals unknown to her were involved in a plot to assassinate President Kennedy and that she would be killed if she gave any information to the authorities." (15)

Jack Ruby, referring to Karen Carlin, stated in a lie detector test that "If there was a conspiracy, then this little girl that called me on the phone in Fort Worth, is then a part of the conspiracy." (16) He referred to her call on the occasion of Sunday morning, November 24, 1963, requesting money, to which Ruby responded by sending her twenty-five dollars just prior to shooting Lee. This could have been done innocently, and I do not want to speculate on what this call meant, as it is just too vague.

Ruby went directly to the police headquarters after sending the money to Karen, made his way through the crowd and murdered Lee, all within a matter of minutes. Karen knew no freedom from fear after that. During the Ruby bond hearing, a jailbreak occurred, and a procession of guards and prisoners rushed right past Karen. She screamed, "Oh, my God, they're after me!" She later made the statement, "I was scared I was going to get killed before I ever got to court!" (17)

This account of Karen reminded me of a saying I heard somewhere: "Anticipation of death is worse than death itself."

Soon after the trial, twenty-year-old Karen Carlin was found shot to death in a Houston hotel, her beautiful body hanging upside down in the shower. She knew that Lee and Ruby were linked together, but she didn't know who the other conspirators were, so she lived in dread, not knowing who her future assailant might be. I knew the conspirators, since I was told who they were, and also I have been able to put the scattered links together.

For the first time, things that were going through Lee Harvey Oswald's mind for a period of time during the summer of 1963, have now been made known. Up until now, there was no proof that Lee confided in anyone except Marina…to a limited extent. He shared many things with me that he never shared with her or anyone else, so there has been no previous record of the many things I am bringing out in this book. I don't know of anyone who ever interviewed Lee Harvey Oswald in a setting where he was open and relaxed, confiding his innermost thoughts and desires to someone he trusted…yet I was able to do this.

Lee hated Russell Long, and it was all I could do to keep him from shooting him. He also wanted to shoot at Mrs. Rose Long because he thought she was backing McKeithen in his bid for governor, although it was actually Blanche Long. Some publications have mentioned that Lee conspired to blow up the Huey Long Bridge on some pretext for anti-Castro elements. He could have had a dual purpose, but he approached me for a different reason. He told me, "If you'll promise to help me hijack a plane to Cuba, I'll blow up the Huey Long Bridge to scare Mrs. Long out of the campaign, then you'll be free to go with me."

I don't know of anyone who has linked Lee with Ruby and lived to tell about it, except for Beverly Oliver. I met with

Beverly in Dallas during the production of the movie, "JFK," and I would like to add that she is still a very beautiful woman. Beverly, Joe Pesci, Tivala Dean and I went out for pizza one evening during the filming of the movie. Tivala's father was chief-of-security at the Dallas police station the day Ruby shot Lee. It was at this time that Beverly said she had witnessed a meeting between David Ferrie, Lee, Jack Ruby and Jack Lawrence. She had sat at the table with Lee, Ruby and her friend Jada, at the Carousel Club some 25 years before. We relayed this information to Oliver Stone, but it was something she didn't like to have broadcast. Beverly was a singer in the Colony Club across the street from Ruby's establishment. She was also known as the Babushka Lady, because at the Kennedy shooting she had on a kerchief tied under her chin, which made her look like a Russian grandmother. At this time Beverly had taken movies of the assassination, and the camera had been confiscated by the FBI immediately following the tragic events at Dealey Plaza.

Beverly, who was quite tipsy that night, became very fearful and stopped sharing information with me as soon as she realized I was writing this book. She made the comment that she had preserved her life by remaining silent. Her friend Janet Conforto, whose stage name was Jada, had talked too freely and this resulted in her death. Beverly said, "The less I talk, the better off I am." She attributed her longevity to her ability to stay silent.

Beverly's testimony corroborates what I have told about the connection between Lee and Ruby, and about Lee's numerous meetings with Ruby during the months of August through October, 1963. Lee strongly opposed the assassination plan up until September 9, and he would have done anything to get out of it until Castro's signal came from Havana. Lee was very angry when I told him of Russell Long's erratic behavior at the Gillis Long rallies, and it rekindled an old hatred that almost left the senator dead.

I told myself I didn't know much about Lee and the assassination, but the truth was…I was afraid to remember. I knew more about it than I wanted to admit. Regardless of what effect this story has on those who read it, the silent voices of those who cry out for justice deserve a hearing.

Another thing that earns its place in this chapter is vital information that will doubtless be of interest to everyone who learns of it. Marguerite Oswald, Lee's mother, stated that she saw a photograph of her son holding a rifle with both hands above his head in a defiant manner. She and Marina had destroyed the photo in order to protect Lee.

I discussed the matter with Priscilla McMillan, who had lived with Marina for seven months while writing her biography. She told me that knowing Marina as she did, she would never take a picture of her husband in such a defiant pose, so it is highly doubtful that Marina took the picture. Indications are that it was Lee's head and someone else's body.

I have examined a backyard photo of Lee, and the body appears to be that of Roscoe White. There is a distinct cut in the photograph where Lee's face is apparently superimposed from the lower lip above. The chin in the photo is square, more like White's, unlike Lee's pointed chin with a cleft. I met Roscoe in person, so I know his stature is a perfect match to the figure in the famous photograph. He stood like that, with his right hip swung to the right, and I can never remember seeing Lee stand like that.

David Ferrie's actual concern over the assassination began

in late 1966, when Garrison initiated the investigation into the matter. He told a friend, "I'm a dead man!" (18) On February 22, 1967, David's body was discovered at his apartment, along with two suicide notes that had been typewritten…including his signature…on both documents. Ferrie's death was a national tragedy because of the information that died with him. When his body was removed from his apartment, many questions were left behind that would forever remain unanswered. David was indeed an interesting individual.

IN THE WAKE OF THE

ASSASSINATION

CHAPTER XVII

News of the assassination spread like wildfire throughout the world, leaving behind a wave of confusion and unrest that is still unsettled three decades later. The failure of the United States government to properly investigate the tragedy and the subsequent cover-up, has resulted in a chaotic atmosphere where truth gives way to skepticism and disgust. Their all-out effort to protect those responsible for carrying out the tragic act and the determination to protect the image of those lend-

237

ing their approval, was truly an insult to the intelligence of the American people!

James Garrison, former district attorney in New Orleans and now a federal judge, conducted his own highly publicized investigation of the assassination during the sixties. The United States government, as well as most of the national media, termed this investigation controversial.

Because of skepticism promoted by national leaders, to protect the image of the government and to dub Lee Harvey Oswald the lone assassin, it has been rightly said that the martyred victim that November day in Dallas was not only John F. Kennedy, but America itself.

I cannot escape my share of blame for not coming forth for the Shaw trial in New Orleans. It has eaten away at me throughout the years, and I have been plagued off and on by ulcers and various other health problems, which I attribute largely to circumstances surrounding the assassination. The guilt has gnawed at me continually, creating a heavy burden that is always with me…no matter where I go or what I do. Unfortunately, no one has ever invented a time machine that would make it possible to go back in time and relive the past, but at some point we can stand up for what is right and try to undo the wrong we have done to the greatest extent possible. This I have made every effort to do by writing this book. America's sacred cow, the Warren Commission, must be exposed!

I was a bit concerned about a television trial that took place in November 1988 that convicted Lee in absentia of being the lone assassin of President Kennedy. This was one of the things that prompted me to write this book, revealing what I know about the assassination. But little did I know how it would be received! This fact has become an important issue to me because I am coming to grips with what an assassination survivor is faced with when coming out of the closet, and I feel this book gives a good deal of insight into that aspect. Unlike many books, it is not authored by an assassination scholar, but by a survivor, which should definitely add to its credibility!

While attempting to promote publicity for this book and establish its credibility, I encountered obstacles I hadn't anticipated from the beginning. These included an attempt to contact authors who have written about Lee Harvey Oswald. I felt they surely would be interested in my relationship with Lee prior to the assassination. I had held this information at bay for so long until it never even entered my mind that I might not receive a response to my letters.

It was a surprise to me that James Garrison never even responded. He had written at least two books about Lee, and was district attorney in New Orleans, as well as prosecutor at the Shaw trial. I met Garrison while working for Oliver Stone in Dallas, and I felt perhaps it was his age that contributed to his lack of response to my letters, since he was getting on up in years. However, when I met him I didn't bring up the subject. Garrison portrays Earl Warren in the "JFK" movie. I thought this man, who was then a federal judge, would be keenly interested in a witness he had overlooked, and one that he knew existed. He referred to this particular witness when he stated in his first book, *Heritage of Stone,* in referring to Lee's change-of-address card, "Who says that lone assassins have no friends?" When I talked to Garrison during the filming of the movie, he appeared not to be well. He told me..."I want to live to finish this movie so the young people will know the truth about the assassination."

Jim Garrison died October 21, 1992. He was a great American who will one day receive recognition for his accomplishments, although he will not be around to see it. Frank Mankiewicz, political aide to Robert Kennedy, made the comment that Garrison will get a share of the credit for the release of secret documents that shed light into the Kennedy assassination. One thing that was hard for me to deal with was that Congress claimed they had thoroughly investigated the matter, so the case was closed even though they established the presence of a second gunman.

Formerly, any newsperson I happened to contact suddenly became incredibly busy with other things, once it had been determined that I was writing about Lee Harvey Oswald! They left me hanging in the wind with my mouth open. This was hard for me to swallow, because in the process of reading books on the subject I found that every time Lee had sneezed, it was made a note of and studied. Now here was a man coming out of the woodwork with startling new information, and it was being treated with indifference! I contacted various newspapers, and was turned away in every instance. I got in touch with several authors who had published books on Lee, but none of them responded to my letters except Priscilla McMillan. This struck me as rather odd, because they had gone to great lengths to gather information, and here it was being offered to them on a silver platter, and they weren't even interested!

My first glimpse of progress came when I contacted Congressman Peter Defazio March 15, 1989 and testified to these events at his office at the federal courthouse in Eugene, Oregon on April 20. What I related to his aide, Jeff Stier, impressed the congressman to such an extent that he sent the report to William Sessions, director of the FBI in Washington, D.C., which any researcher will tell you was an obvious mistake. By that time, I had completed a dossier on the subject, which I sent to Dan Rather at CBS News, and he did not respond either. So much for my earth-shaking news!

I received a letter from John E. Collingwood, inspector in charge of the Congressional Affairs branch of the FBI, and he told me that my report had been referred to their investigative division for information and review. As of this date, I have received no further reply. The government has suppressed vital information that the public is entitled to, which they have had a difficult time gaining access to. Much of it has never been made public, and steps must be taken to rectify this situation!

Priscilla McMillan wrote me a letter in which she told me I had too much to say on the matter to just deal with a vanity publisher, so she contacted the Doe Coover Agency in Medford, Massachusetts. The agency is a Boston-based literary concern specializing in serious non-fiction. My manuscript was accepted, and they agreed to locate a major publisher and take on negotiations for a publishing contract. This agency was a reputable company representing a variety of projects such as the companion books to "Eyes On the Prize," the PBS television series on the civil rights movement in America. However, after much consideration, it was decided the manuscript needed additional work.

It was about this time that I went to work for Oliver Stone, and this afforded me the opportunity for additional research which I was able to use in my book, enhancing its contents. Oliver Stone, producer of "Born on the Fourth of July" and

"El Salvador," became interested in my story. He was in the process of producing "The Doors" at the time. He was also doing research on a proposed production, tentatively entitled "JFK," and I accompanied him to New Orleans, where he went to investigate my story.

Oliver was impressed, so he hired me to be his assistant, serving as technical advisor to the movie. We first went to my old apartment at 1923 Iberville, and took photographs. Except for being a little time-worn, the place still looked the same after twenty-seven years. We went across the street where I had seen Lee walking with his rifle toward the end of August 1963. I remembered there had been a sidewalk in the area, but there was no sign of one then, so we dug under the dirt about three inches and sure enough, the sidewalk was still there!

We then went to 544 Camp Street, where Guy Banister's office and Mancuso's restaurant were located. Katzenjammer's Bar next door was where I had met Guy Banister and David Ferrie that evening so long ago. Both had been replaced by the new federal courthouse, and we were very disappointed to see the changes. Beyond Camp Street Lafayette Square could be seen in the distance, much the same as I remembered it. The park bench I used to sit on was gone and there were not as many pigeons as I remembered. However, there was a concrete bench near the corner of the courthouse on Lafayette, and there was a wino lying on it, fast asleep in the warm New Orleans sun. Looking toward Lafayette Square, one could see the old federal building that housed the post office where I deposited the change-of-address card for Lee. But where was Lee's office? Could progress have stamped it out of existence? I needed to find the indenture that had contained the odor of tires and oil, where many years ago a mechanic could be found, busy at work, changing a tire or tuning up a car.

"Lets walk around the corner to Magazine, Larry," I told Larry Howard, who had accompanied us. After we turned the corner, suddenly there it was…like a cinema in color, the meeting place where Lee and I had spent countless mornings with our shattering revelations, our fears and reassurances! It was the Crescent City Garage, still standing, as if time had forgotten it ever existed. I walked inside, half expecting to find Lee waiting, anxious to tell me about the happenings of the previous day. The same old clock still hung on the wall. The time said ten forty-one, but it was 1990 instead of 1963.

The garage was now being used as a parking facility. The board wall on the left where Lee had hidden his papers was gone, and the office had been moved to the opposite side. Although the sign on the office door still said "Alba," the caretaker was from a new generation.

Stepping out of the garage onto the sidewalk, I showed Larry where I had met Marina in front of the Reily Coffee Company on Magazine Street. Larry spoke up, saying, "Marina lived in the 4900 block, Ron, which could be forty-six blocks from here! It will be very interesting if she can confirm this." And Marina did confirm it, as mentioned elsewhere in this book.

Things were happening fast that day, as we had a lot to do, and a short time to do it in. Oliver was scheduled to catch a plane around four in the afternoon, and this gave us little time for our scheduled interview. In fact, we didn't even have time for lunch. It was decided that I would be seated beside Oliver in the van as we toured some New Orleans historical houses that interested him. Also, on his itinerary was the race track where I learned that even wealthy young movie producers eat hot dogs.

My interview with Oliver Stone lasted a couple of hundred miles. Exhausted, he slept about halfway to the airport. There were seven of us altogether, including Alex Ho, who giggled and whispered all the way to the airport, while Oliver was sleeping.

"Boy, I'm glad he's gone!" the girl driver exclaimed, after Oliver had departed. Then the smokes lit up and heels were plopped onto the dashboard, as they let their hair down, happy that Oliver was no longer on board.

The next thing on the agenda was to take the route that Lee and I had taken in early August. I didn't remember whether we had taken Camp Street or Magazine on this walk, but more than likely it was Camp, because of its closer proximity to Lee Circle and Plaza. I told Larry there was a cemetery we would be walking by, yet we could not seem to find it. However, I later found evidence that a cemetery on Howard Street had been moved. As we came to Lee Circle and Plaza, I told Larry of a girls' school that used to be near there, and a reknowned assassination researcher, Mary Ferrell, substantiated the fact that it had existed in 1963.

We had a problem locating the slaughter house that Lee and I had walked to. Mary Ferrell and Larry Howard kept pointing to a place on the map that was much too far away, but Mary found it in a 1963 New Orleans telephone book. We located it right where I had insisted it was. It was The Viking Packing Company, which was located at 346 Calliope Street, and is no longer in existence.

Next, we took American Airlines flight 135 back to Dallas, where I checked in at the Stone Leigh Hotel. There were three high points remaining during the next three days. We were scheduled to visit Lee's grave, meet with Marina and check

Lee's change-of-address card. I found that each of these acts would arouse a particular feeling of emotion inside me.

At first I experienced a feeling of embarrassment when we located the copy of the change-of-address card, because it wasn't my writing on it! I had printed the required information on the form, and had entered in both the old address on Magazine Street and Lee's post office box number in New Orleans. The new address was 2515 West Fifth Street in Irving, Texas. However, the Magazine address was omitted, so all of Lee's mail must have been delivered to the post office box. The form I had filled out apparently went into the wastebasket. The application the researchers showed me in Dallas in 1990 contained neither Lee's writing nor mine, but was dated October 11, 1963. But regardless, it was I who filled out and deposited the original card, as I alluded to earlier in this book.

I felt a little timid about meeting Marina, and I think she felt the same. However, after our meeting we spent several enjoyable hours together, which included dinner and a pleasant conversation. We discussed things that will always remain private and confidential. I want to thank her for being such a warm and gracious hostess. If all people were like Marina, the world would be a better place in which to live.

Later, I met Lee and Marina's daughters, June and Rachel, on the movie set. In my opinion, one cannot meet the Oswald family and go away without loving them. Months later in Dallas, I talked at length with Rachel, who was born just a month before the assassination. I felt sorry for her, as she was searching for answers. She asked many questions about her father that I wish I had been able to answer. But Lee was a private and complicated person, and even though he and I were close friends and shared many confidences, no one knew him well enough to be able to answer her questions satisfactorily. She was hoping to find he had been everything she longed for in a father, but unfortunately, that was not the case. However, I was able to tell her that to the best of my knowledge, Lee was not as guilty as he appeared to be. I long for the time when the question of Lee's guilt can be cleared up in the eyes of the public, and he will be vindicated in connection with Kennedy's death, especially for Rachel and June's sake.

I would spend the next night at the Great Western Motel in Arlington, not exactly the luxury that had been previously extended to me, but it was close to Lee's grave, and after breakfast this would be our next stop. It was a difficult morning for me, especially when my thoughts kept flashing back to the time so long ago when Lee and I had shared countless intimate moments. I sometimes had flashbacks with visions of Kennedy, lying on his back with his mouth open and his brains splattered everywhere! God, what a pity! I had allowed this to happen without opening my mouth in protest!

Both Larry Howard and his wife, Daryl, attempted to console me, saying, "If it hadn't happened in Dallas, it would have happened somewhere else. Besides, who would you have been able to tell? You knew you couldn't trust the FBI!" But this did not bring me any consolation. I was tormented by the constant thoughts of what I had allowed to happen, and was overcome with emotion so intense that I found difficulty dealing with it…overwhelmed by feelings of guilt and sadness!

In the course of editing the manuscript for this book, my collaborator, carefully questioning me about every detail, stated, "You mentioned how difficult it was for you on the morning you visited Lee's grave, and how Larry Howard and his wife, Daryl, tried to console you. Were you just depressed or did you actually shed tears?" At first I tried to change the subject, since I have always considered it a sign of weakness for a man to cry, and I was ashamed to admit that I had wept. But my collaborator, being a thorough and persistent person, and always determined to make sure all the information in this book was factual, would not allow me to evade the question. "It's not shameful nor a sign of weakness for a man to cry," she told me, with empathy, "Remember...Jesus wept, and he was a perfect man." Finally, although it was a difficult thing for me to do since I am a proud man, I reluctantly admitted to my collaborator that I had indeed cried that morning.

My greatest consolation was that June, Rachel and Marina had survived, and little did they know that if Lee or I had said a word to the wrong person about the assassination, it could have ended their existence, also. Yes, it was a dangerous period we all lived through, but we survived, even though Kennedy and Lee lost their lives. Perhaps this may sound callous...but how many lives does one trade for the life of another? Surely, this question deserves some serious consideration!

By the time I reached the graveyard that day, I had recovered somewhat from the depression that memories of Lee's death and the assassination always brought. As I stood before Lee's grave, I felt that someday I would like to improve the headstone. Rather than simply saying "OSWALD," it would say, "LEE HARVEY OSWALD, BORN 1939, DIED 1963."

HIDDEN PROFILE

CHAPTER XVIII

On a cool morning in December 1990, as I stood beside Lee's grave at the Rose Hill Cemetery, my companion Larry Howard, asked, "If Lee were able to talk now, what do you think he might say?"

"He would probably say, 'What took you so long?'" I replied. With body language, he would have emphasized the word "You" to such an extent that I would have felt it in the pit of my stomach!

This got me to thinking…"Did anyone really know Lee, and truly understand what he stood for? Or do we prefer to believe what the government wants us to believe, digging no further into the matter?"

I was Lee's only friend in America, and I would like you to know the Lee that I knew. I was acquainted with the deep, dark side of Lee Oswald, and as far as I knew, he never killed anyone. He never even admitted killing Martin Schrand. I may have my own thoughts on the matter, but it does not prove anything. As far as Lee's shooting at General Walker, he told me he intended to miss. He had talked of shooting the Longs, but it never came about. And lastly, the paraffin tests revealed that Lee Oswald never fired a shot on November 22, 1963. This shows the strong influence of government propaganda. If Lee were able to speak out from the grave, do you not think he would bring these issues up?

Lee had completed the ninth grade at the age of seventeen, and joined the Marine Corps on October 26, 1956 for a three-year term. After basic training, he went to the naval air station at Jacksonville, Florida. From there, he rode with Martin Schrand to Keesler Air Force Base at Biloxi, Mississippi, where he was trained in aircraft surveillance and the use of radar. Lee was then granted a low-level security clearance. Next he went to the Marine Air Corps Station at El Toro, California, and in late summer of 1957, he was sent to Japan to an air control squadron outside of Tokyo at Atsugi. This was a U2 reconnaissance base where Lee was required to have a security rating. It is interesting to note that Lee had an IQ that was rated 118 on the Weschler scale.

He had an accident with an unauthorized 22-caliber pistol, which landed him in the naval hospital for two and a half weeks. Next he went to Subic Bay at Bataan, in the Philippines, where he experienced firsthand the effects of U.S. military imperialism upon the local Filipino natives. Why should they be forced to shine the shoes of American GIs for a stick of gum or a cigarette? What would they do for a candy bar or a whole pack of smokes?

As Lee kept to himself and silently observed these atrocities, perhaps seeing himself as a boy under similar circumstances, he must have been appalled. We don't have to make a hero out of Lee at this point, as the hungry, half-naked Filipino children scrambled to do favors for these military giants from a prosperous nation. However, we do have to give anyone credit who questioned what was going on there. It's no great wonder that Lee began to sympathize with the opposition to such imperialism.

The opposition happened to be local communists, and communism had been on Lee's list of alternatives for better government. Under such an arrangement his mother would no longer have to work at menial labor to produce profits for capitalists. Yes, Lee was now seeing Americanism at work, and it strengthened his desire to search for a better government. For a while it pointed toward communism. Local communist groups would grow to be a dangerous threat to Corazon Aquino a quarter of a century later. Oliver Stone had been in Viet Nam and had observed the exploitation of the Vietnamese children. In a conversation I had with him I could see that he felt sorry for them, and it was easy for him to understand how Lee would be opposed to the same treatment of the Filipino children. We filmed a scene for "JFK," depicting these incidents.

Martin Schrand, the friend that Lee rode with from Jacksonville, Florida, to Biloxi, Mississippi, was on guard duty one night at Subic Bay, guarding a hanger that probably housed a

U2 surveillance aircraft, a top secret item. Schrand was shot to death that night in a manner that indicated it was not accidental. In 1963 Lee and I discussed that event, and he persistently refused to say whether or not he actually killed Martin Schrand. As previously mentioned, the court ruled that it was an accident, and Lee was content with that verdict.

He returned to Japan with his unit, where he was court-martialed for fighting with a sergeant in a bar. He spent seven weeks in the brig because of the incident. While incarcerated, he was sent out on detail with a group led by an armed guard. He was forced to do many humiliating jobs that he was too ashamed to talk about. He had to GI certain areas, which involved picking up cigarette butts and dumping the tobacco out on the ground. Afterwards, he rolled the paper into little balls and threw it on the ground with the tobacco. In policing the areas, he even had to pick up dog manure and dispose of it with his bare hands. He was also reduced in rank, experienced a forfeiture in pay, and his request for extended overseas duty was denied.

Some of these incidents were never mentioned in any of the books written about Lee, because it was something he was ashamed of and never did make public. I'm surprised it was included in our dialogue in 1963, since most normal people would not want to publicize that they had been forced to submit to such degrading acts. In my earnest desire to inform the public of many undisclosed things that went on in Lee's life, I have related this account just as he revealed it to me.

At this time, Lee's interest in communist publications was stimulated, as he was reading their literature and associating with known communists. It was during this period that he contracted venereal disease in the line of duty. He returned to the U2 base at El Toro, California, where he was assigned to aircraft surveillance. There he studied Russian, mostly on his own. His association was for the most part, with officers instead of enlisted personnel. They would have ordinarily been considered off-limits to enlisted men. He would lure them into discussions beyond that of his apparent caliber. Then when they thought they had him backed into a corner, he showed them up with his wit and knowledge on such matters. This made them appear unqualified as his superiors.

Castro was the subject of a popular issue at that time, and Lee dreamed of joining him in Cuba and becoming a resister of Batista. He was still searching for a better government and had always been disappointed in his quest. Perhaps he thought... "Maybe I'll find it this time!" After he was honorably discharged due to a hardship, he left for Russia on September 29.

The little boy in Lee still showed through his makeup, especially in Russia when he turned twenty. During his first trip to downtown Moscow, he bought an ice cream cone. At twenty-three, when I knew Lee, the boy in him was still evident in many respects. When I met him in New Orleans, we frequently ate a morning ice cream cone from Mancuso's Restaurant. In my capacity as technical advisor to "JFK," Oliver Stone asked me, "What did Lee do for excitement?" I answered, "He probably just ate an ice cream cone." He gave me a quizzical look. I'm sure I could have told him more interesting tales. Things such as electrifying spy yarns, escapades with women, etc., would have sounded more exciting, but this wasn't the Lee I knew.

It took Oliver a while to begin understanding the real Lee. I pointed out to him that simple things could be enjoyed, such as ice cream cones. Oliver and I went to the race track in New

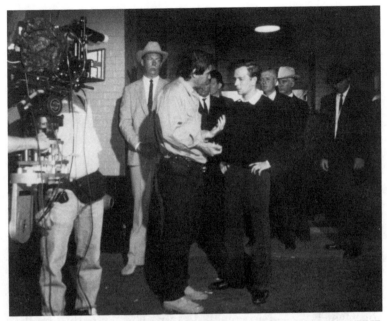

OLIVER STONE ADVISING GARY OLDMAN FOR A SCENE IN THE MOVIE JFK. (20)

Orleans in December 1990. At the concession stand we looked at the exotic menu, and what did Oliver order, but a hot dog! When I commented on this, he was reminded that simple things in life were enjoyable. He was beginning to see another side of Lee's complex life.

Through Gary Oldman, who portrayed Lee Oswald in the "JFK" film, I pointed out the caption in the book *Libra*. It was in a letter that Lee had written to his brother. It read, "Happiness is not based on oneself, it does not consist of a small home, of taking and getting. Happiness is taking part in the struggle, where there is no borderline between one's own personal world, and the world in general." (19) Gary passed this information on to Oliver, adding to his awareness of the real Lee.

While serving as technical advisor I became very close friends with Gary Oldman. He was an excellent choice to portray Lee, as there was a boyish quality in him so much like Lee's. It was quite obvious, though Gary was thirty-three, nine years older than Lee was when he was killed!

While in Russia, Lee expressed a desire to continue his education in economics, philosophy and politics. However, he was not allowed to do this under Soviet policy, since he was a foreigner. Anything Lee learned from this point on would be from the school of hard knocks or from other sources, such as the news media or from certain publications. It was at this time that he became disenchanted with Soviet communism, partly due to the rejection of his application to enroll in the Patrice Lumumba University. He soon learned that in Russia the "glass ceiling" limited his occupation to assembly line work in a factory, which was unacceptable to him. The sky had to be the limit or he would seek a government elsewhere so he could enjoy that freedom.

Lee was disgusted with America, and concluded that things were based on greed. He felt that unemployment and poverty were the end results of such a system. He said America was profit-oriented, in favor of the capitalists, not because it didn't offer any opportunities or precious freedoms, but because those principles in 1963 only applied to certain segments. For instance, he lived in a country at a time when Blacks drank from fountains marked, "Colored," and fountains for Whites were marked, "White only," although the water was no different in either case.

Lee grew up seeing a separation of people sanctioned by the government. He had reverence for the founding fathers, who believed all men were created equal. He had the greatest respect for Abraham Lincoln, and especially John Kennedy, who carried on the struggle for equality.

Lee surely thought that Russia, a people disgruntled with American capitalism, would offer a better government. It took a brave young man to sojourn all alone to a communist giant behind an iron curtain. He soon found that communism was dominated by fear, secret police and regimentation. He had hopes of finding a better government through Cuba or perhaps China. Without doubt, they would have failed Lee also.

I, too, looked for a better government, and for a few years I belonged to a group called "Citizens for Better Government." However, like Lee, I found myself in a distinct minority, and no matter what I did to bring about a change, it didn't even amount to a drop of water in the ocean! I observed a spiritual decline in America. In the fifties I saw people go to jail for illegal cohabitation and sodomy, which are condemned in the Bible. By the seventies, sodomy was the going thing, and courts were even ruling on issues of "Palimony," upholding cohabitation outside of marriage. Now, in the nineties, homosexuals are a legal minority. Those who support this, claiming they have a right to homosexuality under the Constitution, are church-minded people.

I wanted to be a Christian, but I couldn't belong to a church which supported a government that passes laws that scoff at the Bible. Consequently, I became one of Jehovah's Witnesses, who adhere to a theocratic government, and make up a nation called Spiritual Israel. This nation is scattered throughout the world, 4 million strong. The issues Lee was against are resolved by this nation, so I strongly feel that had he lived, he too, would have eventually become one of Jehovah's Witnesses.

While talking with Marina in 1990, I brought up my feelings on the matter, and she replied, "No, Lee would have never become a Witness, because he didn't like people telling him what to do." But she didn't understand that Witnesses are able to make their own choices as long as they conform to the Biblical laws and principles. One thing that Marina and I could agree on was that Lee would not have become a member of any religious organization that supported, or even winked at, any secular, man-made imperfect government. Although Lee professed to be of Christian faith, we can only speculate about his religious preferences, because he was merely in the process of searching, nothing more. I never knew of him to ever enter a church door. We had discussed Christian Science's mind-over-matter, and he was probably more interested in that than anything else. We also discussed Catholicism, which was distasteful to him. I cannot say we never discussed Jehovah's Witnesses, because when taking "Gillis Long for Governor" material from door-to-door, I mentioned to Lee, "I feel like a Jehovah's Witness," and he looked at me and smiled.

Lee discussed political issues with me extensively. However, it is nearly impossible to tell anything new about his political views, as there has been so much written already on the subject, such as the following:

"The key fault of our era is the economic competition between imperialist powers, which leads to wars, crisis and oppressive friction. I call it greed. Runaway automation and the lack of retraining for those who are job displaced because of it, is the offspring of such competition. The movements of all the world's governments leads to a common destruction. Can I turn to factional mutants of existing man-made governments, or to revisionists or existing religions? Never!" (21)

Lee was not without religion, but he detested what man had made of it. Although he despised the hypocrisy of those who claimed to be Christian, he was not down on God. Lee was grateful that God had given him a daughter, June, and would soon give him another child. I recall that he protested the baptism of June, because she was too young to understand what was happening. Marina arranged the baptism without his knowledge or consent, which upset him. To him, it was a ritual without meaning. He said, "If she had been at the age of consent, I wouldn't have protested."

Lee found war distasteful, specifically the Korean and Vietnam wars. He was convinced they were initiated to get the economy moving, to put food on the table, and he detested it. In Lee's eyes, war was profit-motivated toward the Military Industrial Complex. He was deeply troubled about the underlying reasons for American involvement in Viet Nam. Yet, legally speaking, under Soviet policy, America was his only route out of the Soviet Union, and it was the land of opportunity, where he could presuppose his own ideas.

Lee felt that in order to ward off the destruction imperialist powers would bring upon one another, somebody must stand up and oppose the governments, the people, the land and the foundations of the society from which they sprang. (22) Lee could accept tradition if it were progressive, but when it produced negative effects he was in opposition. For example, the difference between Gillis Long politics and Russell Long politics, the way he saw it, was that Gillis was progressive and Russell was negative. I wholeheartedly agreed with him.

Lee had lived under two governments, and he liked certain things about both, "...but, he opposed their basic foundations." (23) Capitalism was based on greed, and Soviet communism was based on fear. He said that the new system he fostered must be opposed to the old. The old was made up of war, crime, racial barriers, injustices, poverty and so on, but he said no system can be entirely new. (24)

Alix Taylor gave an analysis of Lee's character. I spent hours on end with Lee, discussing these matters, and I can assure the reader that at least some of her words described the Lee I knew:

> "He disliked Russia very much. He didn't agree with communism and he didn't agree with capitalism. Lee desired a perfect government, free from the many problems experienced today. He wanted to live under conditions where everyone's needs were provided, and there was no taxation or discrimination, no need for law enforcement of any kind. He longed to do exactly as he pleased, whenever he pleased, enjoying total and complete freedom in everything. He believed in no government at all, just a perfect place where people lived happily together." (25)

Lee feared any form of government that resembled a police state. Alix Taylor's analysis continued, but the rest doesn't give an accurate description of Lee. He realized police involvement was necessary for such a perfect arrangement, and that the troublemaker had to be dealt with. However, if no other man was capable of creating such a perfect place in some six-thousand years of civilization, would it be logical to think that Lee could do so?

It wasn't possible for him to find the paradise he had searched for in this system while men exercised rule over men.

We have to give Lee the credit that is due, because he stood for something better. He searched for perfection, which man has been unable to bring about, as attested to by the historical record. When Lee was killed, he was denied the opportunity to defend his actions. Who knows what the final outcome of Lee Oswald would have been, if he had lived?

In March 1992 I was invited to Washington, D.C. by George Paige Associates to appear on a nationally televised show, entitled "JFK Conspiracy; Final Analysis." My purpose on the program was to elaborate on Lee and his connections with Guy Banister and Jack Ruby. Each member of the panel was interviewed by host James Earl Jones, providing the opportunity for much vital information to be presented. After interviewing Victor Marchetti, assistant to the former Deputy Director of the CIA, the interview began:

James Earl Jones:

"Oswald was a very mysterious person. To find out more about him, we have asked Ron Lewis, a friend of Oswald's, to join us tonight. Oliver Stone, the director of the movie "JFK," told us about Ron and his book called "Flashback, the Untold Story of Lee Harvey Oswald."

Oliver Stone:

"Marina Oswald confirmed to me that Ron Lewis did exist and she remembered him because he bumped into her one day in New Orleans when she followed Lee to work."

A fast-forward version of events was shown from the assassination to the murder of officer Tippit. The actual events covered three-quarters of an hour. Afterwards, Jones continued with the interview, which eventually ended as follows:

> "Mr. Lewis, you said earlier that Oswald was involved in a plot to kill Kennedy. Was Oswald supposed to kill Kennedy?"
>
> Ron Lewis:
> "He knew there was a plot to kill Kennedy, but he didn't want anything to do with it. But eventually he became involved with them."
>
> James Earl Jones:
> "Who was supposed to kill Kennedy?"
>
> Ron Lewis:
> "He told me Roscoe White was supposed to kill Kennedy. He was supposed to be one of the trigger men.
>
> James Earl Jones:
> "Thank you, Mr. Lewis."

I am happy that I had the opportunity to bring out some facts on the show, including Lee's acquaintance with Ruby, and the fact that White acted as one of the trigger men in the assassination. Also, I was able to verify Lee's ties to the 544 Camp Street address. This testimony should not be taken lightly nor shrugged off as another theory or hoax, because I was there and saw it happening.

In my efforts to present the truth about what really happened that fateful day in Dallas, November 22, 1963, and the events leading up to it, I have pursued every means at my disposal. I have contacted the news media, testified to a congressman, acted as technical advisor for Oliver Stone's movie, "JFK," appeared numerous times on television, and lastly, I

VICTOR MARCHETTI, JANET TURNER AND RON LEWIS IN WASH-
INGTON, D.C. (26)

have written this book.

I realize I do not have signed affidavits from the conspirators, but honestly, can one expect such under the circumstances? All I can do is relate this account truthfully exactly as
it happened. My only proof that I knew Lee Harvey Oswald
died with him, and with others who knew of our relationship,
except for Marina Oswald Porter's admission that she remembered seeing me when I bumped into June's stroller in front
of the Crescent City garage. Also, proof lies within the Banister files under my alias, Ron Larson, which can be verified if
the files are ever located.

I have related this story truthfully, just as it happened.
Whether you accept or reject it, it's your prerogative, as you
have the freedom to make that choice. You have read it; now
judge for yourself.

EPILOGUE

Since Mark Lane, in his book *Plausible Denial,* has named Gerry Patrick Hemming as part of the conspiracy and cover-up, it prompts me to tell what I know about Gerry. First of all, I want to say that he is my friend. Whatever he might have done will never affect my feelings for the Gerry Hemming of today.

He may have been a different person in 1963. Lee and I had conversations about him, and we knew he had worked for the CIA. We discussed a photograph of Gerry that appeared in a New Orleans newspaper in 1963 when he was apprehended by the U.S. Coast Guard on a hit-and-run mission against Cuba. Lee told me he had served with Hemming in the Marine Corps.

Previously, I said there were two men who had accompanied Lee, Ferrie and Ruby, on the trip to the blimp base to transfer armaments, and I was informed that they were large men. Gerry is six feet, eight inches tall and weighs 260 pounds, and I believe he was one of the men I was unable to identify. I met him in 1991 when I was working with Oliver Stone on the "JFK" movie, and we became buddies, hanging out together. He gave me his Miami phone number and address.

Gerry was especially knowledgeable about the transfer of arms that had taken place at 544 Camp Street. For a scene in the movie I dressed a group of Cubans in a combination of military and civilian clothing so they could be transferred with arms, to the secret training base in the swamp near Lake Pontchartrain. Gerry accompanied them in battle dress.

My impression of Gerry is that he is a very nice person. Could he have been one of the trigger men who shot the president, as indicated by Mark Lane? Gerry told me in a private conversation that he had been to Banister's office, where he loaded munitions for transfer to the training camp. On the movie set I called on him to help me prepare the building directory in Banister's office for filming. His memory of several details indicated that he had been there many times before. There were things he mentioned that only he and I knew about, things that had never been published. Without a doubt, Gerry Hemming was deeply involved in the conspiracy scenario.

When I met the Dallas researchers in 1990, they had some

things to say about Priscilla McMillan. I was told she was a CIA agent who had hindered their investigations by holding up the Marina Oswald biography for many years. They felt she did this on orders from her superiors. Priscilla told me that one researcher, who shall remain nameless, had pestered her for years about this. "It has been one of the dark spots in my life," she told me. Priscilla is my friend, and I feel empathy for her because of the unkind things the Dallas community of researchers said about her. Needless to say, I do not share their sentiments, and Priscilla's eventual contribution is invaluable. Mark Lane names her as a conspirator, and God knows she is innocent of anything of that nature.

I received a letter from Priscilla, dated December 6, 1991, in which she stated, "No, I never worked for the CIA, and no, I didn't hold up my book on anybody's orders." And I believe her.

DEFAZIO, INSTRUMENTAL IN GETTING
FILES RELEASED:

I am elated that my efforts to work with Oregon Congressman DeFazio have been well-spent. I received a letter from him dated February 19, 1992 which read:

> *I have introduced two pieces of legislation to remove the shroud of secrecy around the evidence. The first measure would make available for public use all records of the House Select Committee on Assassinations immediately upon the adoption of the resolution. The second directs the Archivist of the United States to immediately make available for public use all records of the Warren Commission.*

He also said, "I believe that if there is nothing to hide, then hide nothing."

This is, of course, not the final word. There is the matter of the Banister files, confiscated by the FBI in 1964 after Guy Banister's death. This is where the conspiracy unfolded, at 544 Camp Street in New Orleans. An effort to release the files is the first step in getting the Kennedy case reopened. The thanks for the DeFazio legislation should go to the critics of the Warren Commission. They were labeled "buffs" to make them appear as hobbyists who play with model toys or collect dolls. These people cried out recently and their voices were finally heard. Some of these were able to express their sentiments recently at the premier of the movie "JFK" in Eugene, Oregon. It was just a typical location and a typical audience, but it was interesting to note their reactions. A reporter for the

Eugene Register-Guard, Jeff Wright, was on hand to get the comments from viewers, and I have included a portion of his article, as follows:

"Several viewers said the film confirmed their suspicions, but also left them feeling depressed and powerless. 'It's very disturbing!' twenty-five-year-old Tanya Hansen said. 'It gives me a kind of overwhelming and helpless feeling.' Another viewer, Ed Johnson, thirty-five, stated, 'I feel kind of duped.' Johnson said he remembered his fourth-grade teacher crying on the day of Kennedy's murder. 'It's a scary feeling-very Orwellian.' Seventeen-year-old Monica Bosserman said she 'had her suspicions' about the CIA after learning about the intelligence agency in a high school history class. The film, she said, validated her skepticism. 'What kind of a future are we going to have?' she asked. 'You can't have faith in the media, in the Pentagon, and in the White House. It leaves you feeling that no matter what happens, you can't do anything about it. It's all so corrupt!'

"Bosserman's date, nineteen-year-old Mike Pitzer, said the film impressed upon him how people must look out for themselves, because they can't rely on the system. 'I hoped to find some truth, and I found out a lot of truth I never knew before,' he said. Enid Smith was even more emphatic. 'It's incumbent upon every American to see this movie, and open themselves to the possibility of its truth, and then act accordingly.'"

These grass-root-level reactions are in sharp contrast to those aimed at Mr. Stone by high-level media supporters of the *Warren Commission Report,* such as the Washington Post. These film viewers should not be ignored. After all, people such as these are what make up America. Because of the bungling and cover-ups involved in the assassination investigations, we can no longer have confidence in high-level commissions whose conclusion is cut-and-dried at the outset. The only hope of solving the crime of the century, lies within the grasp of the common people.

The writers of this book invite comments from the readers, especially those named therein. They will make every effort to acknowledge all correspondence and may be contacted at the following address:

Ron Lewis
P.O. Box 158
Winchester, Oregon 97495

INDEX

1. *Conspiracy,* Summers, Shapolsky
2. "Hands Off Cuba" leaflet, "JFK" movie, Ron Lewis photo
3. Katzenjammer's Bar, "JFK" movie, Ron Lewis photo
4. *For Your Eyes Only,* Fleming, Burkley Publishing Corp.
5. *Marina and Lee,* McMillan, Harper and Row
6. *Legend of Lee Harvey Oswald,* Epstein, Random House
7. *Legend of Lee Harvey Oswald,* Epstein
8. *Crime of the Century,* Kurtz, University of Tennessee Press
9. "Four Days", Heritage magazine
10. *Marina and Lee,* McMillan
11. *High Treason,* Robert Groden, The Conservatory Press
12. *Examining the Scriptures Daily,* Watchtower Bible and Tract Society
13. *Legend of Lee Harvey Oswald,* Epstein

14. *Marina and Lee*, McMillan
15. *Contract on America*, Scheim, Kensington Publishing Corp.
16. *Contract on America*, Scheim
17. *Contract on America*, Scheim
18. *Heritage of Stone*, Garrison
19. *Libra*, DeLillo, Viking Publishing Co.
20. "JFK" movie photo, Ron Lewis
21. *Marina and Lee*, McMillan
22. *Marina and Lee*, McMillan
23. *Marina and Lee*, McMillan
24. *Marina and Lee*, McMillan
25. *Marina and Lee*, McMillan
26. "JFK" Conspiracy photo, Washington, D.C.

APPENDIX

1. I received the following letter from Robert W. Oliver, Assistant to Governor Atiyeh, of Oregon, dated September 17, 1979:

> *I am happy to inform you that Governor Atiyeh has granted you a full and complete pardon with respect to the offense of which you were convicted in 1950. Appropriate action has been taken with respect to your police records. This pardon relieves you of any disability you might have had under state law."*

There are people who believe that at this time, because of my upgrade of military discharge and pardon, I was separated from the Central Intelligence Agency, something that was purely speculative. my ten years' disappearance when I could not be contacted, probably contributed to such a rumor.